GOLDENDOODLE: GOLDENDOODLES OWNERS BIBLE

GOLDENDOODLE PUPPIES, MINI, GOLDENDOODLE BREEDERS & RESCUE, OWNERS GUIDE, PRICES, ADULTS & FULL GROWN SIZE, TRAINING, GROOMING, HEALTH & MORE.

By Susanne Saben

© DYM Worldwide Publishers

DYM Worldwide Publishers

ISBN: 978-1-911355-52-6

Internet. The accuracy and completeness of the information provided herein and opinions stated herein are not guaranteed or warranted to produce any particular results, and the advice or strategies, contained herein may not be suitable for every individual. The author, publisher, distributors, and/or affiliates shall not be liable for any loss incurred as a consequence of the use and application, directly or indirectly of any information presented in this work. This publication is designed to provide information in regards to the subject matter covered. The information included in this book has been compiled to give an overview of the topics covered. The information contained in this book has been compiled to provide an overview of the subject. It is not intended as medical advice and should not be construed as such. For a firm diagnosis of any medical conditions, you should consult a doctor or veterinarian (as related to animal health). The writer, publisher, distributors, and/or affiliates of this work are not responsible for any damages or negative consequences following any of the treatments or methods highlighted in this book. Website links are for informational purposes only and should not be seen as a personal endorsement; the same applies to any products or services mentioned in this work. The reader should also be aware that although the web links included were correct at the time of writing they may become out of date in the future. Any pricing or currency exchange rate information was accurate at the time of writing but may become out of date in the future. The Author, Publisher, distributors, and/or affiliates assume no responsibility for pricing and currency exchange rates mentioned within this work.

Table of Contents

Resource List

This quality resource list will help you further maximize your experience with the Goldendoodle breed. Enjoy!

Breeders USA (in Alphabetical order)

- **Adorable Down East Labradoodles**
  http://www.adorabledowneastlabradoodles.com/ - Arizona, California, Maine, USA
- **Almond Blossom Doodles**
  https://www.almondblossomdoodles.com/ - Central Valley, California, USA
- **Angel View Doodles**
  http://www.angelviewdoodles.com/ - Birmingham, Alabama, USA
- **Apple Creek Doodles**
  http://www.applecreekdoodles.com/ - Clyde, Michigan, USA
- **Asha's Doodles**
  http://www.ashasdoodles.com/ - Fremont, California, USA
- **ASD Companion Doodles**
  http://www.asdcompanionlabradoodles.com/ - Sacramento, California, USA
- **Beyond Bliss Doodles**
  https://beyondblissdoodles.com/ - Evan Mills, New York, USA
- **Big Dog Labradoodles**
  http://www.bigdoglabradoodles.com/ - Central California, USA

- **Coastland Goldendoodles**
  http://www.coastlandgoldendoodles.com/ - Ventura, California, USA
- **Cliberdoodle**
  http://www.cliberdoodle.com/ - Goodrick, Michigan, USA
- **Cutiedoodles**
  http://www.cutiedoodles.com/ - Brentwood, Northern California, USA
- **Doodles of Autumn Hills**
  http://www.doodlesofautumnhills.com/- Greenbrier, Arkansas, USA
- **Four Star Dood Ranch**
  http://www.fourstardoodranch.com/ - Dallas, Texas
- **Laurel Ridge Goldendoodles**
  http://laurelridgegoldendoodles.com/ - Virginia, USA
- **MorningShine MountainDoods**
  http://www.doodlesofvermont.com/ - Vermont & New York, USA
- **My Doodle Darlins**
  http://www.mydoodledarlins.com/ - Morrilton, Arkansas, USA
- **Moss Creek Doodles**
  http://www.mosscreekgoldendoodles.com/ - Central Florida, USA
- **Petit Jean Puppies**
  https://www.petitjeanpuppies.com/ - Oppelo, Arkansas, USA
- **Smeraglia's TeddyBear Goldendoodles**
  https://www.teddybeargoldendoodles.com/ - Robertsdale, Alabama, USA

- **Stardoodles**
  http://www.stardoodles.com/- Pinson, Alabama, USA
- **Timshell Farm**
  http://www.timshellfarm.com/ - Happy Jack, Arizona, USA
- **Virginia Beach Goldendoodles**
  http://www.virginiabeachgoldendoodles.com/ - Virginia, USA
- **West Shore Doodles**
  http://www.westshoredoodles.com/ - Ludington, Michigan, USA

BREEDERS CANADA (IN ALPHABETICAL ORDER)
- **Burkhart's Kennels**
  http://www.burkhartskennels.com/ - Wallenstein, Ontario, Canada
- **Goldendoodles of Niagara**
  http://www.goldendoodlesofniagara.com/- Ridgeville, Ontario, Canada
- **Parkridge Goldendoodles**
  http://parkridgegoldendoodles.com/ - Cobble Hill, BC, Canada
- **Ruff'n Ready Doodles**
  http://www.ruffnreadydoodles.ca/ - Magrath, Alberta, Canada
- **Snowy White Doodles**
  http://www.snowywhitedoodles.com/ - Vancouver Island, BC, Canada

BREEDERS UK (IN ALPHABETICAL ORDER)
- **Kizzabella Doodles**
  http://www.kizzabelladoodles.co.uk/ - UK
- **UK Goldendoodles / Jastra**
  http://www.ukgoldendoodles.co.uk/ - UK

Introduction

Man's best friend, trusted companion, helper, protector and even confidante—these are but a few of the ways we think of our beloved pet dogs.

That said, it could surprise you to know that dogs, as we have come to know them, descend from a mysterious, potentially dangerous and, frankly, scary canine called the gray wolf.

Nobody knows for sure when or how it happened, but virtually everybody agrees that the domestication of the gray wolf benefited those who were brave enough to do it, the gray wolves that were nice enough to be tamed, and the rest of mankind. Indeed, we have had very capable help with hunting, herding, and protection against bad elements in the domesticated wolves. In return, we've kept them fed, sheltered and safe.

A man's best friend, trusted companion, and protector, the Goldendoodle is a beloved pet dog.

Why did we choose the gray wolf for domestication? They are as social as people, so they made for great companions. Wolves, in general, are particularly social animals. Like us, they tend to live in groups, called packs, that have a hierarchy. For example, some wolves rise to become leaders of their respective packs, or claim the leadership, much like we do when we find ourselves in a group. Being so didn't make it difficult to train them to recognize us as their leader. In the numerous years that passed since the first gray wolves were domesticated, more breeders appeared and altered the canines to suit their needs or preferences. Some bred them to be smaller, cuter, etc. This is why we now have more than 400 dog breeds.

The Goldendoodle is currently one of the most popular dog breeds. Many consider it to be the perfect companion dog. This is because it possesses three of the most sought after canine characteristics. They have a: friendly, loving, energetic and playful temperament, above-average intelligence which makes it easy to train, and good looks brought about in large part by its adorable coat which can be soft or silky and curly, wavy, shaggy or straight. It's also best suited for people who have allergies since its coat is also relatively hypoallergenic. Thus, it would most probably be a surprise to only very few people that you have chosen a Goldendoodle to be your new fur baby, buddy or addition to your family.

Currently the most popular dog breed, the Goldendoodle is considered man's perfect companion.

Deciding to make a Goldendoodle part of your life is as exciting, fun and rewarding as it is a big responsibility. Ever heard of the saying that getting a dog is like having a child? This is because both require major adjustments in one's life for the bond to be created the right way. You need to prepare by reading up on as much as you can about the Goldendoodle, dog-proofing your house, and getting the proper supplies, which include good dog food, grooming tools, and training tools. You also need to learn which type of Goldendoodle is right for you, how to recognize a trustworthy breeder, how to spot a good pup or adult dog, how to take care of your new pet and how to train it.

Look no further. All the information you'll need is right here in this book.

CHAPTER 1

Goldendoodle History: What is the Origin of the Goldendoodle?

Shaggy but in an irresistible, oh-so-cute way. With small but surprisingly expressive eyes, a delightfully kissable nose and floppy ears which bob while it plays, like pennants waved by a happy child—it is no surprise to us that you have chosen a Goldendoodle as your new pet.

That soft, warm, fleece-like coat, those tiny peepers just barely able to peek through that veritable curtain of fringe fur, yet able to convey volumes of emotions, that stand-out whiffer (a slang term for nose) that hones in, digs into and nuzzles almost everything it comes across with unabashed enthusiasm. This is sure to place you under a spell that will make you want to love this dog to bits.

*Before getting one, it may be good to get know the history
and origins of Goldendoodle.*

To help you get to know your new buddy as well as possible, this chapter teaches you about the origin (i.e., history) of the Goldendoodle dog breed. To be specific, you will learn about where Goldendoodles originally came from, as well as how and why the pioneering Goldendoodle breeders bred the Goldendoodle. You will also learn what a 'designer dog' is, and why Golden Doodle dogs are sometimes called designer dogs.

Where Did Goldendoodles Come From?

Goldendoodles were first bred in the early to mid-1990s in North America and Australia. This was done as an attempt to create guide dogs that were suitable for people who had visual impairments and allergies, like asthma and hay fever.

Also called service or assistance dogs, guide dogs are dogs that are trained to help those who are visually impaired get around safely. For example, they can lead their humans around obstacles.

Breeds that are trained as guide dogs are chosen based on several criteria, most important of which are trainability and temperament. Nowadays, the German Shepherd, the Labrador and the Golden Retriever are the breeds that are most often chosen to be guide dogs by service animal facilities, followed by the Australian Shepherd, the Border Collie, the Collie, the Visla and the Standard Poodle.

Currently, the Labrador Retriever is the most popular breed employed as guide dogs around the world. There are various sizes of it to choose from, keeping it well-groomed is fairly easy due to its short coat, it is generally hearty, it is gentle, and it is easy to train.

How and Why Did the First Goldendoodle Breeders Breed the Goldendoodle Dog?

Among the visually impaired who also have allergies, the hybrid of (or cross between) the Golden Retriever and the Standard Poodle—the Goldendoodle—is the most popular guide dog because it combines the Golden Retriever's desirable qualities with the Standard Poodle's nonshedding coat along with many of the Standard Poodle's other desirable qualities.

The Golden Retriever is a big dog breed. They were breed to serve as 'gun dogs,' or dogs that were trained to retrieve waterfowl (e.g., ducks) and upland game birds that were shot down by hunting or shooting parties. Because they can retrieve game in one piece, the dogs are also called retrievers. They possess an inherent love of water, are easy to train, and have long coats that consist of a thick inner coat that provides them with sufficient warmth when it is cold and an outer coat that lies flat against their body, letting them repel water. They are well suited to both suburban and country environments. While they need a lot of regular outdoor exercise to stay healthy, they need to be kept in a fenced area because of their instinctual penchant to wander. They shed a mess of fur, particularly when the season changes, so they need regular grooming to stay looking as well as possible. They are among the popular breeds trained to become guide dogs because they are so amiable. They are so friendly and gentle, that they are among the top five of the most popular family dog breeds in the USA, as well as among the top ten of the most popular family dog breeds in the UK and Australia. They also are not picky eaters and are very playful.

The Goldendoodle is the most popular guide dog because it combines the Golden Retriever's desirable qualities with the Standard Poodle's nonshedding.

Ranked as the most intelligent dog breed second to the Border Collie, the Poodle is known for being very skillful. It performs exceptionally well in many sports and activities for dogs, including obedience, agility, tracking, and herding. This is why they do very well as assistance or service dogs. The three main sizes that they have been bred are Standard, Mini and 'Toy.' The Standard Poodle is the oldest variety and was later bred down in size into the Miniature and Toy Poodles, according to the American Kennel Club, which officially recognized the breed in 1887, along with The British Kennel Club. But the Miniature and Toy Poodles were developed within only a brief period after the Standard Poodle became recognized as the general type.

In the past, Standard Poodles were trained as hunting and working dogs. The Miniature and Toy Poodles were bred mainly for companionship, but there were some reports that they also may have been popular as truffle-hunting dogs because their paws were small and therefore less likely to cause damage to the fragile fungi when they came across it. The unusual fur shapes, proportions, and colors that some Poodles were seen sporting back then was a trend that began in the mid- to late-19th century among Victorian and Georgian women. This lead to the breed becoming recognized as the dog of the middle- and upper classes.

Goldendoodle: Its name is the portmanteau of the shortened word 'golden' from the Golden Retriever dog breed's name and the Poodle dog breed's shortened name.

Like the Golden Retriever, the Standard Poodle, the largest Poodle variety, was traditionally employed as a gun dog. This Poodle variety has served as such since the early '90s in both the USA and Canada. The modern Standard Poodle still possesses most of the traits sought after by the original breeders and early owners, including: a sharp working intelligence that lets it carry out commands easily, webbed paws that make it an agile swimmer, a love of water similar to that of the Golden Retriever, athletic stamina, and a moisture-resistant coat that acts like a wool jumper, enabling the dog to stay warm, dry and comfortable in damp conditions.

In the second half of the 19th century, Poodles were employed less and less for hunting because they were employed more in more in circuses as well as a status symbol of the rich. This is why they were seen mainly as circus and companion dogs in the 20th century. But in the past couple of decades, some American and Canadian breeders have been selecting Standard Poodles with a drive for birds to redevelop them as hunting dogs, including the American Kennel Club in 1998 and the Canadian Kennel Club in 1996.

They succeeded in the third quarter of 2014, when they redeveloped some Standard Poodles as hunting dogs that were highly intelligent, having an aptitude second only to the Border Collie; had lightning quick reflexes; very eager to please their masters; pursued their quarry relentlessly; were strong swimmers; had a keen nose; and had an excellent memory.

This is why the Standard Poodle was also employed since the 17th century as a working dog in the military. During WWII, according to Roland Kilbon with *the New York Sun*, certain countries employed dogs in their respective armies, and have been doing so for many years.

Eventually, with the approval of the American Kennel Club, the Professional Handlers Association, Seeing Eye, Inc., and obedience training clubs across the country, Dogs for Defense, Inc., a nationwide program, was initiated and became the official procurement agency for all war dogs employed by the Army, Navy and Coast Guard. It obtained the dogs that the Army trained. In 1942, the Army officially classified the Poodle as one of the 32 breeds trained as 'war dogs.'

Meanwhile, the Miniature and Toy Poodles became widely successful as small, relatively hypoallergenic family pets. This, then, inspired Golden Retriever breeders to cross a Golden Retriever with a Standard Poodle to try developing a larger, relatively hypoallergenic family pet. Thus, the Goldendoodle is sometimes called a 'designer dog.'

Why Is the Golden Doodle Dog Sometimes Called a 'Designer Dog'?

Also called crossbreed dogs, designer dogs are dogs that have been intentionally bred from two or more recognized, purebred dog breeds that were not artificially bred enough to become and be recognized as purebred breeds.

According to the *Encyclopædia Britannica,* the term 'designer dog can be traced back to the late 20th century, when breeders began crossing purebred Poodles with other purebred breeds to develop a breed that had the Poodle's relatively hypoallergenic coat, its desirable traits and the desirable traits of the other breeds. This means the Goldendoodle is among the first designer dog breeds.

The main identifying mark of a designer dog breed is its name that is a portmanteau, or a word that is a combination of two words. In the case of the Goldendoodle, its name is the portmanteau of the shortened word 'golden' from the Golden Retriever dog breed's name and the Poodle dog breed's shortened name.

Other examples of designer dog breed names are:

- Schnoodle, which is a portmanteau of the shortened Schnauzer dog breed's name and that of the Poodle's

- Shepsky, which is a portmanteau of the shortened word 'shepherd' from the German Shepherd dog breed's name and the shortened word 'husky' from the Siberian Husky dog breed's name

There are other purebred breeds that are being crossed to develop designer dogs that have a virtually endless range of labels, like the Puggle, which name is a portmanteau of the Pug dog breed's name and the shortened Beagle dog breed's name. There are also more complex designer dogs, with multiple breeds from recent ancestry, that are being named this way, like the German Chusky, which name is a portmanteau of the word 'German' from the German Shepherd dog breed's name, the shortened word 'chow' from the Chow Chow dog breed's name, and the shortened word 'husky' from the Siberian Husky dog breed's name.

Are Labradoodles and Goldendoodles the Same?

In the last three decades, Poodle crosses have become quite popular. Indeed, the Goldendoodle dog breed's name was first used in the early '90s, in the USA, several years after Wally Conron (the man who is credited with developing the Labradoodle dog breed) coined this dog breed's name.

Labradoodles were developed to serve as guide dogs for the visually impaired who had allergies. In the late '80s and '90s, their popularity skyrocketed among assistance, service and companion dog owners, prompting breeders to cross Golden Retrievers with Standard Poodles, to find out if the former's gentle and cheerful nature and the latter's high intelligence and relatively hypoallergenic coat could produce a cross as popular as the Labradoodle.

Thus, the Goldendoodle was redeveloped and became popular.

That said, contrary to what many assume, while they may look the same and have a somewhat similar sounding name, Goldendoodles and Labradoodles are different dog breeds.

Both Labradoodles and Goldendoodles are very well-tempered and make great family dogs.

However, Labradoodles are not as friendly as Goldendoodles. For example, Labradoodles will hesitate to crawl up to you to say hello, get to know you, and make friends with you. In other words, they are shy around strangers or others dogs. They are not sociable compared to other breeds. Even if you do not keep a close eye on them, they will not get so excited that they will get out of control and like leap onto guests. This is because they tend to be standoffish in the company of strangers or in new environments. They stay at a distance and observe until they have gotten used to the new people, pets, place or situation.

For example, when you have a guest over, and you own a Labradoodle, expect the dog to stay at the opposite end of the room and intently watch the newcomer for several minutes before crawling up to the newcomer to say hello and get acquainted.

Unlike Goldendoodles, Labradoodles are not particularly energetic. They are not openly enthusiastic, so they do not come across as lively, passionate dogs. This is because they are less excitable. They tend to be quieter.

This does not mean they are dull or lazy dogs. They just not as zesty as Goldendoodles.

Both the Goldendoodle and the Labradoodle make terrific family dogs because they are mild mannered, but Labradoodles make better guard dogs than Goldendoodles because, generally, they are more protective.

That said, while some consider this as one of the Labradoodle's positive traits, there are those concerned that the Labradoodle's protective nature could cross the line into being aggressive. This could not be further from the truth because Labradoodles are not known to be aggressive.

Labradoodles are better guard dogs than Goldendoodles does not mean they are good guard dogs. Generally speaking, Labradoodles and Goldendoodles do not make proper guard dogs because they are far too friendly compared to most other breeds. In other words, they are not effective watchdogs.

For instance, you cannot count on either of them to bark at newcomers as they come up to your home loudly and intimidatingly. They will just stay quiet and make friends with your guests once they are inside.

Apart from being a little larger, the physical differences between Goldendoodles and Labradoodles are in their coats. Labradoodles' coats tend to be a bit shorter and more wiry, while that of the Goldendoodle is longer and wavier. Most of the difference in their coat is because of the differences among their generations.

For example, first- generation Goldendoodles have wavier coats than F1B, or second, generations. They also shed more.

Since they are friendlier, more affectionate and more patient with strangers and kids, Goldendoodles have become increasingly employed as domestic pets. Possessing the Poodle's prodigious intelligence and the Golden Retriever's easy trainability, Goldendoodles are not only becoming more and more popular in the USA, the UK and Australia, but they are also now employed in services other than hunting and being guide dogs, including being therapy, search and rescue dogs.

CHAPTER 2

Golden Doodles Characteristics: What Sets the Goldendoodle Dog Breed Apart?

N ow that you have learned all about the Goldendoodle's history, let us get to know the breed itself more. This chapter tells you the differences between the F1b Goldendoodle, the F2 Goldendoodle, the F2b Goldendoodle, and the English Goldendoodle; the colors of the Goldendoodle's coat (i.e., black, apricot, red and chocolate) and how you ought to choose; and the Goldendoodle's sizes (i.e., the average size and weight of males and females in general, as well as the average size and weight of the Mini/Toy/Petite/ Teacup Goldendoodle). This chapter also tells you all about the Goldendoodle's temperament to help you adjust to yours.

A Goldendoodle at play!

How Do the F1b Goldendoodle, the F2 Goldendoodle, the F2b Goldendoodle, and the English Goldendoodle Differ from Each Other?

To best discuss the differences among these variations of the Goldendoodle, let us begin with the **F1 Goldendoodles** or the **First Generation Goldendoodles.** They are the first-generation crosses, which basically means they are the direct, first offspring of the original Golden Retriever and the original Poodle that were selected. As such, they enjoy the health benefits associated with 'hybrid vigor.' This refers to the phenomenon in animal breeding where the first cross of two unrelated purebreds grows healthier and therefore better than its parents.

First-generation crosses are precisely 50 percent of each of their parents. In other words, half of their chromosomes came from one parent, and the rest came from the other. To get a clear mental image of how this plays out, imagine a normal cross' 78 chromosomes as 39 black marbles and 39 white marbles in a large bowl with each color representing its parents. When it reproduces, its sperm or egg will contain randomly picked 39 marbles. Statistically, the mixture will be somewhat distributed evenly. But it is possible that 39 black marbles get picked, producing a purebred of either parent.

The level of maintenance needed by the coat of F1 Goldendoodles ranges from moderate to high. The typical length their coat can grow ranges from 3 to 5 inches and are normally curly or wavy, so they only require combing and occasional grooming to stay looking great. Some have shorter coats, but they are rare. Generally, they shed very little. Combining this with their relatively hypoallergenic coat, they are perfect for a family who has mild allergies.

Next in the family tree are the **F1b Goldendoodles** or the First-Generation Backcross Goldendoodles. They are crosses bred back to one of their original breeds. Generally, they are crosses of a Goldendoodle bred to a Poodle. On average, this makes them 1/4 Golden Retriever and 3/4 Poodle. As such, they do not have as much hybrid vigor as F1 Goldendoodles. But they are still quite hearty.

Like F1 Goldendoodles, F1b Goldendoodles' coats require moderate to high levels of maintenance as their fur can grow up to the same average length and are just as curly or wavy. They also do not shed as much. They are, however, recommended for families suffering from moderate to severe allergies because their hypoallergenic coats have been improved as compared to F1 Goldendoodles.

Unlike F1 Goldendoodles and F1B Goldendoodles, **F2 Goldendoodles, or Second Generation Goldendoodles,** are crosses of two Goldendoodles. They are the least common Goldendoodle variety because they are the most genetically varied, making them unpredictable. To solve this, breeders employ an F1B Goldendoodle because the pups have more of the original purebreds' genes, making them more predictable. But doing so does not eliminate their unpredictability, so the level of maintenance their coat needs, their respective coats themselves and the amount of fur they shed varies. This said, they are not recommended for families with allergies.

Last, but certainly not the least, is the **English Goldendoodle.** It is a cross between a Poodle an English Golden Retriever. The English Golden Retriever is recognized as the original Golden Retriever breed that came in 1868 from Scotland. They typically have a very light coat, a somewhat boxy head, and are calm compared to the Golden Retrievers that were developed in the USA and some parts of Canada.

How to Choose Between the Black, Apricot, Red and Chocolate Goldendoodles

The differences among Goldendoodles do not stop at the ways that they were bred. Next are the colors of their coat that can be black, apricot, red or chocolate.

Labrador Retrievers, Golden Retrievers, Poodles, Goldendoodles and other similar breeds have two pairs of genes that determine the color of their respective coats. These are B/b and E/e. Their coat's shade, or how light or dark their respective coats are, can be modified by other genes that they possess. These are V/v and R/r.

With the Goldendoodle you would choose to have at least one B and at least one E, he or she will have a black coat. The combinations BbEE, BBEE, BBEe and BbEe, produce the same result. To be precise, a dog that has the BbEE combination will have a black coat but will have the recessive brown gene; BBEE produces a black coat and produces no recessive gene; BBEe produces a black coat and produces the recessive cream gene; BbEe produces a black coat and produces either the recessive cream or recessive brown gene.

Generally, a **black Goldendoodle** should stay solid black. In other words, its coat should not fade or turn silver, or gray. There are black Goldendoodles that have the recessive gene that can prematurely gray their fur.

Any Goldendoodle that has 'ee' will have a cream coat, which refers to white, cream, apricot, red, yellow and golden. To be precise, BBee produces a pure cream coat; bbee produces a caramel coat, or cream coat with some brown pigment, and Bbee produces a cream coat and the recessive brown gene. The shade can also be modified by other genes.

An apricot Goldendoodle's fur is similar in color to the inside of a peach. Many apricot Goldendoodle's coats fade, while some deepen in color.

A red colored Goldendoodle's fur is similar in color to the Irish Setter's. The coat of some get highlighted over time but stay a deep red overall.

All Goldendoodles with bb and at least one E will have a chocolate, or brown, coat. To be precise, bbEE produces a chocolate coat; bbEe and bbEE produce a coat with some chocolate pigment, and bbEe produces a brown coat and the recessive cream gene. Just like the two previous colors, the shade of Goldendoodles with chocolate coats can be modified by other genes.

Chocolate Goldendoodles can stay rich and dark in color or fade. If yours does fade, it should remain a chocolate color, ranging from milk to dark chocolate.

What You Need to Take into Consideration When Picking Out a Goldendoodle Size

After choosing which color suits you, you need to choose which size is the right one. There are several to select from. Apart from the average Goldendoodle puppy and adult heights and weights, there is the Mini/Toy/Petite/Teacup Goldendoodle's average height and weight.

Let us tackle Goldendoodle puppies first. Males and females range from 6" to 15" in height. The average height is 10" to 11" for both. Females can weigh from 5 lbs. to 24 lbs. The average is 9 lbs. to 10 lbs. for them. Males can weigh from 3 lbs. to 27 lbs. The average is 11 lbs. to 12 lbs. for them. When the males grow up, they can reach up to 2' to 2.2' in height at the shoulder. The female adults can reach up to 1.8' to 1.9' in height at the shoulder

Also called Toy Goldendoodle, Petite Goldendoodle and Teacup Goldendoodle, **The Mini Goldendoodl**e is the cross between a Mini or Toy Poodle and a Golden Retriever. Its size ranges from 13 to 20 inches in height. It can weigh between 15 and 35 pounds.

The Goldendoodle Temperament

The last thing you need to learn about a Goldendoodle to truly get to know it is its temperament, or character.

As we have mentioned already, the Goldendoodle has been a very successful family and companion dog. This is because it possesses several sought-after traits.

To begin with, **the Goldendoodle is very affectionate, especially with its adopted family.** While some breeds are independent and aloof even if they have been raised by the same person or people since they were pups, the Goldendoodle bonds closely to the person or people who mainly cared for them while showering their entire family or families with love.

The Goldendoodle is great with kids. Being so does not mean Goldendoodle's are just gentle with them. This also means they are tough enough to stay cool under heavy-handed petting and hugging, as well as in the midst of running and screaming kids.

The Goldendoodle is very friendly with other dogs. Unlike other breeds that attack or try to dominate other pets, or fight with them, or turn tail and run off and hide, the Goldendoodle would rather play with other dogs he or she meets.

The Goldendoodle is particularly friendly with strangers. While many breeds are indifferent, shy, or aggressive around strangers, the Goldendoodle can be expected to be affable— wagging tail, nuzzling nose and all—with newcomers.

The Goldendoodle is very playful. Many breeds normally tend to be quiet, serious or sedate. Not the Goldendoodle. Seemingly a perpetual puppy, it is always up for a game (or two).

The Goldendoodle is quite energetic. Since it is a breed that was originally bred to be a working dog, the Goldendoodle is usually brimming with energy. They naturally possess the stamina to put in a full day of work. Having all this vitality, it is always ready and waiting for some action, like a chase or a game of fetch, so they are more likely to spend time playing, like jumping around, or investigating new sights or smells.

Since the Goldendoodle is a high-energy dog, **it needs a lot of exercise.** While certain breeds will be fine with just a bit of exercise, like an evening stroll around the neighborhood, the Goldendoodle needs plenty of exercise every day. Otherwise, it will put on weight and vent in undesirable, even destructive ways, like barking incessantly, chewing at your furniture or digging in the yard.

The Goldendoodle is very intelligent. It was bred in part for hunting, which requires high intelligence to do complex tasks, like concentrating, decision-making and herding livestock, so the Goldendoodle is highly intelligent compared to most other breeds.

Since the Goldendoodle is a very smart dog, **it needs more mental stimulation than most other breeds.** When they used to be hunting dogs that ran and chased after prey virtually every day, Goldendoodles got the physical and mental workouts they needed to stay healthy. Since it is not common anymore to breed them as such dogs, you should figure out how to give them the mental stimulation they require. If you do not, they will get it on their own—even at your expense.

Since it is a sharp dog, the Goldendoodle is more capable of easily forming the right connections between a prompt, like the word sit; the corresponding action; and the reward, like getting a treat, than most other breeds.

The Goldendoodle is very easy to train. Since it is a sharp dog, the Goldendoodle is more capable of easily forming the right connections between a prompt, like the word sit; the corresponding action; and the reward, like getting a treat, than most other breeds. Other dogs need more time, patience and repetition to get it right. There are breeds that can with relative ease, but unlike the Goldendoodle, they approach training with only the reward in mind. In other words, they are only concerned with what is in it for them, like getting the treat or having fun, rather than get better as a working dog.

The Goldendoodle is not 'mouthy.' This means it does not tend to nip or gnaw. Other breeds, on the other hand, need to use their mouths to hold things or herd their pups. Unlike the Goldendoodle, they need training to learn that nipping and gnawing are allowed only with their chew toys, not you and other people and pets.

Domesticated Goldendoodles do not possess the so-called 'prey drive.' The earlier Goldendoodles were bred to hunt, so they had the innate desire to chase and sometimes take down other animals. Domesticated Goldendoodles had this instinct bred and trained out of them, so you do not need to worry about yours going after other pets in the neighborhood that could look like prey aside from cats, like smaller dogs, hamsters, and birds.

Given all its positive traits, **the Goldendoodle is perfect for newbie dog owners.** Since it is friendly, affectionate, patient, keen and most important of all, easy to train, first-time dog owners will have a fairly easygoing time training a Goldendoodle. Not only that, Goldendoodles are resilient. They bounce right back up from a mistake, so even if the going gets rough, new dog owners can rest assured that getting it done will not be overly difficult.

Despite having several virtues, just like any other breed, the Goldendoodle is not perfect. It has certain traits that you might be concerned about.

For one thing, **the Goldendoodle's tendency to bark and howl is average.** If you would still go for a Goldendoodle even if you know this, check how it barks and howls, as well as how often. Is the sound tolerable or grating? If you live in a place with plenty of wildlife, will the animals send your new dog into a barking and howling frenzy each time they make so much as a peep? Do you live in housing that imposes noise restrictions? Do you have sensitive neighbors? If you would say yes to any of these, you may want to reconsider getting a Goldendoodle.

The Goldendoodle's tendency to wander off is also average. Some breeds are more free-spirited compared to the rest, bred to go far and wide. If given a chance, they will race after virtually anything that catches their eye, like a squirrel that darted across the path. They include the Goldendoodle. If its instinct to roam is going to be an issue for you, you might want to consider a different dog.

Since Goldendoodles like the outdoors, are energetic and are social, they do not adapt well to living exclusively in an apartment. Even the Mini/Toy/Petite/Teacup Goldendoodle will have a hard time being cooped up in an apartment despite being small, so you ought to pick a different breed if you live in a high-rise.

CHAPTER 3

Finding a Goldendoodle for Sale: What are the Things I Need to Look Out For?

N ow that you have been formally introduced to the Goldendoodle dog breed, it is time to find the one that will be your new furry friend for life.

There are several things you need to look out for to pick out the right one for you. To help you make the best choice, this chapter will teach you how to find and recognize good Goldendoodle breeders as well as how to spot a bad Goldendoodle breeder. You will also learn how to choose between Goldendoodle adoption and Goldendoodle rescue here.

To identify a reliable Goldendoodle breeder, you need to know what makes a good dog breeder.

How Do I Find and Recognize Good Goldendoodle Breeders?

To identify a reliable Goldendoodle breeder, you need to know what makes a good dog breeder.

If the breeder is truly worth his salt, he treats his work as a way to celebrate the breed he specializes in.

There are several ways an honest-to-goodness breeder's passion manifests itself in his work.

- **He can demonstrate having extensive knowledge of the breed,** including its history, traits, and temperament. One way is being able to give you sound advice on taking care of your new pet. The breeder cannot if he does not really know as much as he should about the dog.

- **He provides you with guarantees that cover the dog's possible disease(s) or temperament issue(s).** This means you can rest assured you won't have any such problems because he evaluates the health of all his puppies through sound, standardized genetic testing (e.g., hip x-ray certification (OFA); Canine Eye Registry Foundation (CERF); hip joint laxity (or penn-hip); and subaortic stenosis, a heart defect common in popular dog breeds), minimizing his risk of producing a sickly puppy.

- **Requires you to spay or neuter the puppy.** This shows his genuine concern for the dog's well-being. It ensures you will not be forced to take care of any unwanted puppies which could end up as strays, in a pound or in a shelter.

- **He does his best to breed the best dogs possible.** For example, he takes part in dog shows, like competitions, to showcase his dogs. Such events have them competing in obedience trials, sports, and athletics, putting their desirable physical and behavioral traits on display. If the breeder did his job of breeding his dogs as well as possible, they would be able to exhibit the sought-after characteristics of their breed. Participating in dog shows also lets the breeder see if there is any room for improvement among his dogs, enabling him to make improvements if needed.

- **He always puts the welfare of the puppies first.** In other words, he always does what is best for them. For instance, if a puppy shows potential to grow up into a strong or even famous show dog, but the breeder knows the puppy will be better off living with a family as a pet instead, he will ensure the puppy finds a loving home, including visiting a prospective buyer for an interview as well as make sure the buyer can provide a good home. If things still don't work out, he could take the dog back or find another family or home for the puppy.

How Do I Weed Out a Bad Goldendoodle Breeder?

Just because a Goldendoodle breeder has all the qualities we mentioned does not mean you can trust him right away. A bad Goldendoodle breeder who is also determined to deceive unwitting buyers can make himself seem legit. To avoid getting duped by such a con artist, here are ways to spot one.

- **He 'specializes' in various dogs.** No matter how good he claims to be, a breeder who offers a lot of dogs cannot possibly guarantee that he is an expert in them. Not only is there so much to learn about each breed, breeding itself is a learning process, with new information being obtained and new best practices being constantly invented. So, realistically, a breeder can only truly become an authority on one breed.

- **He sells too many dogs.** It is obvious that he is just in it for the money if he does. He does not care about maintaining quality by breeding only in numbers he can really handle— only to make as much cash as possible. He clearly does not care about the consequences, like the possibility that the undesirable pups could be abandoned.

- **He does not stop even if there is a risk of breeding puppies that will be in poor health.** Avoiding this requires testing the puppies' parents, siblings and other relatives for health or behavioral problems. Doing so cuts into the money he could get, so he skips this critical part of the process—putting each litter he breeds in danger of being unhealthy.

- **He keeps cutting corners.** The lengths he might go to keep his costs low does not stop at testing the puppies' parents, siblings and other relatives for health or behavioral issues. He could only feed them cheap dog food that is not very nutritious or not take them to the local vet to get dewormed, vaccinated, checked up or tested further if needed—adversely affecting their health even more.

- **He sells exclusively to or through pet stores.** This shows he does not take the time to ensure each pup is taken into by a loving family, or that he even cares at all. As we have mentioned already, a good breeder personally screens families or individuals looking to buy a puppy (or a few), advises them on how to take care of their new pet(s), and takes back or finds a new home for the ones that get returned.

- **His establishment is in poor condition.** If he has his own place but keeps the dogs he sells in a dirty, crowded or depressing environment. It is unlikely that he takes good care of them; if he does at all, he could be passing onto you the issues your new pet could be suffering from.

- **Does not, will not or 'cannot' show you the puppy's parents, or at least the mother.** You need to check their health, physical characteristics and disposition as those of the puppy will be the same. If they are unhealthy, have less than desirable physical traits and have a poor disposition, their puppy will have the same issues. **At the very least, the breeder should be able to provide you with a certification attesting to the good temperament and health of the puppy's parents.**

- **Does not, will not or 'cannot' show you the puppy's medical history,** including whether the puppy has had its shots, whether it has any potential genetic abnormalities and the vet who checked these. Not knowing this puts you at risk of having a world of problems if your puppy becomes very sick because you will not be able to refer to his or her medical history to know what to do.

- **Does not, will not or 'cannot' provide you with any references for satisfied customers.** You cannot know for sure whether you are getting a quality pup without such references because you cannot double-check whether the breeder does offer reliable puppies.

- **Does not get to know you as much as possible.** For instance, he pressures you to make your decision as quickly as possible. If he does not show any interest in your plans for your new pet, or does not show any concern about whether you know how to raise and take care of the puppy properly. You ought to look for another breeder who makes you feel welcome, lets you to take your time picking out your new fur baby, and allows you to come back as many times as you need to make your choice. Only then will you able to pick out the best Goldendoodle for you.

How Do I Know which to Choose between Goldendoodle Adoption and Goldendoodle Rescue?

Checking out a Goldendoodle breeder establishment or pet store is not the only way you can get a Goldendoodle. You can also consider Goldendoodle adoption or Goldendoodle rescue.

Goldendoodle adoption refers to the option of adopting a Goldendoodle that usually happens when a family cannot take care of the dog anymore and want to find a new good home for your Goldendoodle. Normally attached to their pet, they would rather not place the pet in a shelter.

Advantage of Adopting a Goldendoodle

You can get the dog's complete background. Since the dog's past owners are directly involved in the entire adoption process, you can easily find out the dog's full history including the dog's health, condition, temperament and complete veterinary records. Simply ask them for it.

Knowing not only lets you know for sure whether you are getting a good dog, you will also know what future issues you might have with your furry pet, so you can deal with them.

Disadvantages of Adopting a Goldendoodle

1) Some owners do not know their pet's complete history. Without this history, you will have no idea whether the dog has issues with its health, condition, temperament or behavior until you have your dog checked.

2) Most former owners refuse to take back their dogs. If you found out that your new pet has problems with its health, condition, temperament or behavior and its former owner does not take this puppy back when you try, you will be stuck dealing with your dog's complications.

Usual Requirements for Adopting a Pet

1) **You have to be at least 18 years old.** You have probably heard it many times already, but it is worth telling you again since it is so important. Having a pet is a big responsibility. You have to take care of it 24/7, including feeding it, walking it, bathing it, playing with it and taking it to a vet if it gets sick. Pulling this off requires maturity. 18 is widely recognized as the age of officially becoming an adult, so consider having a pet only when you are old enough.

2) **Have a valid ID**, like a driver's license. You will need it to prove you are old enough to have a pet. It will also be needed to check your background.

3) **Make sure you will be allowed to have a pet of the breed and size you like where you live.** If you live in an apartment, you might not be allowed to have a pet at home, so check if you do not know to avoid having problems with the landlord.

4) **Make sure you have enough time and resources to take care of your new pet,** including medical attention, training, toys and treats.

5) **On the day of the adoption, make sure you have the right transport to take your new pet home comfortably and safely, as well bring enough money to pay the adoption fee if you are charged.**

Goldendoodle rescue refers to the practice of volunteer Goldendoodle foster care groups, who provide a safety net for rescued Goldendoodles. They take in strays, the excess from shelters and pounds, as well as the unwanted Goldendoodles from private individuals. They keep the dogs in their own kennels or homes and put them up for adoption.

4 Traits of a Trustworthy Rescue Group

1) Requires you to undergo an in-depth screening process, including asking you potentially personal questions. While this can be intimidating, the more the group knows about you, the better their chances of matching you to a suitable pet. It is also a great opportunity for you to size them up and find out whether they are legit.

2) Helpful. To find the Goldendoodle that will suit you, not only should a bonafide Goldendoodle rescue group be willing to discuss your expectations, lifestyle, and requirements; they should also address your concerns, answer any questions you have and offer advice on how to take care of your new pet.

3) Committed. To be precise, they show a real interest in the life-long welfare of your new pet. For example, they state in your adoption contract that you may take back your pet to them if things do not work out between the two of you.

4) **Responsible not only for you and your pet but also the rest of the community.** For example, they spay or neuter the dog themselves.

Advantages of Taking in a Rescued Dog

1) **Normally, rescue dogs have been carefully evaluated for health, condition, and temperament.** Depending on the dog's condition, foster care lasts for at least two weeks and up to two months before the dog is put up for adoption. This not only gives the foster family enough time to evaluate the dog's behavior in various situations but also lets them have the dog undergo basic obedience training.

2) **Rescued dogs are usually spayed or neutered.**

3) **Adoption contracts for rescued dogs typically let new foster families or individuals return the dogs.**

4) **Rescue groups are not only more than happy to make the adoption process as smooth as possible but also help prepare owners for their new pet.**

Disadvantages of Taking in a Rescued Dog

1) **Not all rescue groups know the entire history of their rescued dogs.**

2) **There is no guaranteeing your adoption will push through.** Rescue groups screen new foster families or individuals very carefully. They normally require a visit and interview before placing the dogs.

To improve your chances of getting the Goldendoodle you like, make sure you understand all the rescue group's requirements for your new pet (e.g., a fenced-in yard).

To ensure taking in a rescued Goldendoodle goes smoothly, find a rescue group you trust and can build rapport within the Animal Rescue Directory.

CHAPTER 4

Choosing Goldendoodle Puppies or Adults: Which Do I Take Home, a Goldendoodle Puppy or Adult?

O nce you have found a reliable Goldendoodle breeder, or have chosen which between Goldendoodle adoption and Goldendoodle rescue suits you, you can go ahead and choose the Goldendoodle you would like to have as your new pet.

To make sure you pick the right one, this chapter will teach you how to recognize a quality Goldendoodle puppy on offer, as well as how to tell if you ought to go for a Goldendoodle adult.

You will also learn the common Goldendoodle health issues here to help you know what to do if your furry buddy gets sick.

A Goldendoodle with his doctor. A healthy Goldendoodle has regular visits to the clinic.

How Do I Spot a Quality Pup from Goldendoodle Puppies for Sale?

The easiest way to recognize a quality Goldendoodle puppy is by how good it looks.

Begin checking with the pup's coat. It can be the same as his or her Poodle or Golden Retriever side of the family. If he or she took after the former, his or her coat will be tight and curly. It can also be cream, golden, red/apricot, chocolate or black. If he or she took after the latter, his or her coat will be soft and silky. It can also be light cream, golden or coppery red.

The next thing to check is the pup's size. While it depends on the genetic background of his or her parents, it is primarily determined by his or her Poodle side of the family. If his or her Poodle parent is a Mini Poodle, he or she will be small. If his or her parent is a Standard Poodle, he or she will be the same size when he or she grows up.

Some Golden Retrievers are bred to be larger than the breed's standard size. If the Golden Retriever parent of the Goldendoodle puppy you like was bred this way, expect your pup to also be big when he or she grows up.

Once you have settled on the type and color of the coat as well as the size you like, observe how the pup you are considering to have as your new pet behaves.

To find out if the pup is a good dog, observe how the pup interacts with you. If the puppy has been kept with its litter, observe its interaction with its siblings and other puppies as well.

If you approach the pup you like, and it runs up to you, while this could almost seal the deal, keep your cool.

Energetic and daring puppies are virtually irresistible. They are not afraid to jump all over people and start wrestling with them, or grab onto their pants and tug while making cute, tiny growls. They are a lot of fun. But after a few days of having them at home, no matter how adorable they are, they can drive you crazy if they are too unruly. They can also be hard to train.

The more polite and gentler puppies, on the other hand, are unlikely to give you such problems. And just because they do not appear as small bouncing balls of seemingly boundless energy does not mean they will not be as fun to have as pets as livelier puppies. They just need more time to get to know you and get comfortable with you to open up.

You need to spend more time checking out the puppies and do so diligently. Observe the litter instead of going straight for the pup that catches your eye. You will see how he or she behaves around her siblings and other puppies. That will give you a good idea of how he or she will behave at home.

Interaction and socialization are crucial for a puppy's well-being. Generally, puppies are naturally social creatures. After all, dogs are pack animals. It is instinctive for them to form packs that have a solid hierarchal structure. In their respective pack, each pup learns 'the rules,' like their place or roles. Having such experience and knowledge, they grow up into well-adjusted puppies that will not be a problem to take care of.

To find out if the pup you fancy will be a well-adjusted pal for life, watch the litter closely.

Which one or ones are noisy, friendly, pushy? Which one or ones are quiet, mellow, meek? Which one or ones take all the toys and wins all the games? Which one or ones appear delicate? Which one or ones do the rest pick on?

Normally, puppies are outgoing, inquisitive and trusting. They mill about peoples' feet, tug at their shoelaces. They will try to leap onto or crawl into their lap; bite, gnaw or nibble playfully on their fingers; or just wander checking everything out.

If there are four and most or all of them stay at arm's length or bark suspiciously at you, they are most likely a very risky litter.

Shy puppies, like ones that tuck in their tails or shrink away from people, grow up to be shy adult dogs. They are not a good choice to have as a pet especially if you have a child or children. If a puppy's shyness is genetic, it cannot be trained out of your puppy and will grow into a shy adult dog no matter what you do to prevent this. Once grown up, the dog can be hard to live with. For instance, the dog might defensively snap if startled or frightened.

Be careful even if one of the litter appears normal. The puppy could have inherited the same shy or distrustful genes from one of his or her problematic parents or both, and those genes are yet to manifest.

But if you are sure the entire litter is fine, you can move on and observe the pup you like. To not get distracted, ask the breeder if you can see the puppy individually. This is crucial because the puppy can behave differently on their own, which is their normal behavior.

Some puppies act boldly only because their siblings or friends are there to back them up. When they are shy puppies, they are actually friendly and open up when they are away from their more dominant siblings or friends. Some lively puppies dial down their energy when they are alone and not egged on by other puppies.

An ideal puppy to have as a pet is neither bossy nor timid. In other words, he or she has a balanced temperament. Such a puppy will not have the problems that come with having an extreme temperament, making him easy to raise, take care of, and train. Overly shy puppies can grow up into 'fear biters.' They can bite if startled or frightened. This will be problematic especially if you have kids. Litter bullies have dominance issues that will make them difficult to train. A puppy with a balanced temperament plays with other pups and shows interest in his or her surroundings.

You can do a simple aggression test to see whether the puppy you like has a good temperament. Just roll your puppy onto his or her back and gently stroke or scratch his or her belly or chest. He or she will struggle a little as he or she tries to turn himself or herself right back up. But as you keep gently stroking or scratching his or her chest or belly, he or she should calm down and relax. Once he or she does, remove your hand. If he or she has a mainly calm temperament, he or she will stay calm and relaxed for a few seconds before flipping himself or herself over and running off to play some more with his or her siblings or friends. If he or she has a mainly aggressive and dominant temperament, he or she will not relax and keep struggling until you let go.

You can also ask the breeder for the puppy's pedigree. Having a quality pedigree means the puppy's ancestors, including his or her parents and grandparents, had good health, temperament, and abilities. The puppy will also have these choice traits, ensuring he or she is a quality pup.

You cannot find out a puppy's pedigree with his or her pedigree registration papers alone. These just identify his or her ancestors. They are not a guarantee that he or she has desirable traits. In fact, even the titles in a pedigree do not attest to good health or temperament of a dog. Only a reliable breeder can provide such information, and often with supporting documents.

If the pup you are interested in is less than 8 weeks old, check whether it was taken away from his or her mother. Puppies that were taken away from their moms and littermates before they turn 8 weeks of age do not grow up into well-adjusted dogs. They cannot bond well with others, making it unlikely that they will get along with you, other people and other pets.

The last thing you need to check before getting the pup you like to make sure he or she is a quality pup is whether he or she has received the proper medical attention. Has he or she had a detailed checkup? Was he or she cleared by the vet? Has he or she received his or her first round of shots? Has he or she been treated for worms? Ask for a detailed vet record to find out. You will have to deal with these on your own if you find out when your puppy gets sick.

How Do I Know a Goldendoodle Adult Is the Right One?

If you would choose Goldendoodle adoption or Goldendoodle rescue or would go for an adult Goldendoodle rather than a puppy, you will have to make your choice among Goldendoodles with much more characteristics than just being adorable— making choosing much harder.

To know for sure the one you like is the right one for you, make sure his or her size and abilities suit your lifestyle or meet your needs or expectations. Also, think carefully about whether you have the right resources to take care of this puppy properly.

If you live in an apartment or a relatively small house, like a flat, you ought to go for a Mini/Toy/Teacup/Petite Goldendoodle. He or she will not need a lot of space growing up. But if you have a lot of space, including a yard, you can consider going for a standard-size Goldendoodle or even a large one that was bred from a large Golden Retriever.

If you have plans of participating in shows or competitions, make sure the Goldendoodle you would choose can perform as a show dog. He or she should be able to do tests on the sport for dogs of your choice (e.g., obedience, agility or hunting).

To be sure that the Goldendoodle you like can be a show dog, apart from being reputable, the breeder should be a regular and avid participant in dog shows and competitions. This means he or she breeds females that have proven performance records, the requisite health clearances and pedigrees with outstanding parents. This also means he or she breeds them to accomplished males with a titled line, as well as knows how to select pups with the sought-after qualities. Thus, virtually all the Goldendoodles the breeder has on offer are quality dogs.

To make sure you will not have any major problems with your Goldendoodle, also check his or her health and temperament.

Do Goldendoodles Have Health Issues (e.g., What Is the Life Expectancy of the Goldendoodle?)

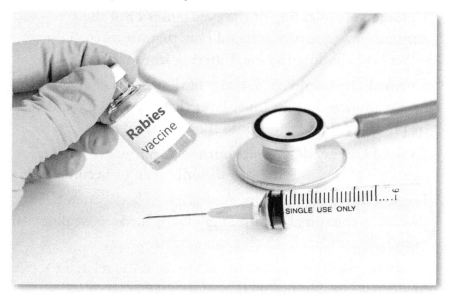

A regular visit to the doctor is a must to maintain the health of your Goldendoodle.

While Goldendoodles are generally healthy, in their average life span of 10 to 15 years, they can have some health issues. Many of these are genetic, resulting from having genes from Poodles and Golden Retrievers. In other words, they may have health conditions common to their pure breed heritages. Your Goldendoodle could be particularly at risk if you were not careful where you got the furry friend from.

The common conditions and diseases documented among Goldendoodles are:

- **Allergic dermatitis, or Atopy.** An itchy skin disease among animals caused by an allergy to irritants in the environment.

- **Cataracts.** A clouding of the eyes' lenses or of their surrounding transparent membrane that obstructs light, effectively blinding the one suffering from this.

- **Corneal Dystrophy.** A disorder of the cornea characterized by a malfunction in its inner layer that keeps it dry and clear by pumping fluid from it into the eye's front chamber.

- **Cranial cruciate ligament rupture.** A rupture of a knee ligament that causes the dog to suffer pain or become lame.

- **Degenerative myelopathy.** A progressively degenerative disease of the spinal cord that gradually leads to weakness and eventually renders both rear legs useless.

- **Diabetes mellitus.** A disease of the pancreas related to inadequate insulin production.

- **Distichiasis.** A condition characterized by abnormal growth of extra eyelashes from the upper or lower eyelid glands that adversely affect sight.

- **Hair loss as an adverse reaction to a subcutaneous injection of the corticosteroids class Glucocorticoids.**

- **Ectopic Ureter.** An abnormal routing of one of the ureters, the tubes that take urine from the kidney to the bladder, causing incontinence.

- **Elbow dysplasia.** The abnormal development of certain elbow joint parts during growth.

- **Entropion.** A disorder characterized by inward rotation of the eyelid, causing the eyelashes to rub against the cornea.

- **Epilepsy.** A disorder characterized by seizures that manifest between the ages of 2 and 5.

- **Skin allergies** triggered by a variety of food ingredients.

- **Gastric torsion, or bloat.** A sudden, life-threatening illness that causes the stomach to get filled with air and twist.

- **Glaucoma.** A disease of the eye that occurs when the pressure within increases.

- **Hemangiosarcoma.** A type of cancer that can affect the liver, spleen or heart.

- **Hip dysplasia.** A malformation of the hip joint that causes pain, arthritis, and lameness.

- **Hyperadrenocorticism.** A disorder that makes the adrenal glands overactive and secrete excessive cortisol that leads to illness.

- **Hypertrophic Osteodystrophy (HOD).** A disease that mainly affects young, large dog breeds that cause their bones to become inflamed, eventually rendering them lame.

- **Hypoadrenocorticism, or Addison's Disease.** Insufficient steroid production.

- **Hypothyroidism.** A condition characterized by an underactive thyroid gland that cannot make enough thyroid hormone to keep the body running normally.

- **Immune-mediated hemolytic anemia.** An immunity disorder that causes the destruction of red blood cells.

- **Insulinoma.** A malignant tumor in the pancreas that secretes excessive amounts of insulin that will lead to hypoglycemia if left untreated.

- **Interdigital Dermatitis.** Also known as pododermatitis, this is inflammation of the paws.

- **Intervertebral Disk Disease.** A disorder that affects the spinal disks, causing pain and difficulty walking that can lead to paralysis.

- **Iris cysts.** Cysts that form in the iris and ciliary body.

- **Hemophilia.** A condition characterized by excessive bleeding.

- **Laryngeal Paralysis.** A disorder affecting the larynx that paralyzes it, causing it to create noisy, difficult airflow into the trachea.

- **Limbal Melanoma.** A type of cancer that affects the eye.

- **Lipomas.** Benign fatty tumors that develop in the subcutaneous tissue.

- **Lymphosarcoma, or lymphoma.** A malignant cancer that affects the lymphoid system.

- **Mastocytoma, or Mast Cell Tumors.** Malignant tumors that can develop in the skin or body.

- **Myasthenia gravis.** A rare condition where transmission of nerve impulses to the muscles are impaired, weakening them.

- **Osteochondrosis Dissecans (OCD).** A condition resulting from abnormal cartilage development.

- **Patellar luxation.** Abnormal dislocation of the patella, or kneecap.

- **Perianal Fistula.** A painful opening in the skin around the anus.

- **Progressive retinal atrophy (PRA).** A disease of the nerve cells at the back of the eye that causes them to degenerate. This usually occurs in older pets and can lead to blindness.

- **Sebaceous Adenitis.** A hereditary skin disease.

- **Squamous Cell Carcinoma.** A type of cancer that originates in the squamous epithelium, a single layer of flat cells. It may appear as a white skin mass or a raised bump on the skin.

- **Von Willebrand's Disease.** A deficiency of the von Willebrand's Factor (vWF), one of the elements that allow blood clots to form.

- **Osteochondrosis.** A developmental disorder that affects medium and large, rapidly growing dogs where abnormal endochondral ossification of epiphyseal cartilage in the shoulders, elbows, stifles and hock joints occurs.

- **Seborrhea.** A skin condition characterized by dandruff as well as greasy skin and fur.

- **Diabetes.** A lifelong condition characterized by abnormally high blood sugar levels.

- **Hot spots.** Also called Summer Sores and Moist Dermatitis, this is a moist, raw skin disorder that can appear seemingly spontaneously anywhere on the body and rapidly deteriorate the surrounding area. It has a variety of causes, but the most common are bacteria.

CHAPTER 5

Preparing the House for Your Goldendoodle: What Are the Things I Need to Do?

After choosing between a Goldendoodle puppy or adult to have as your new pet, you ought to wait before taking your pet home. You need to prepare the house first. There are several necessary changes to be made to ensure your new fur baby can adjust. This chapter will serve as your guide. Here you will learn how to Goldendoodle-proof your home, how to choose the appropriate dog food and the must-haves to take care of your new buddy. There are also some gifts you can consider giving your Goldendoodle to welcome them into your life.

How Do I Goldendoodle-Proof My Home?

Even if you try your best to keep a close eye on your Goldendoodle, you can't always keep tabs on your pet. You have to go to work, buy groceries, spend time with friends, etc. Being on guard can be especially difficult if you got yourself a puppy. The small, energetic, curious little thing can slip into and through almost anything. To keep your new pet safe, you need to make several adjustments to your home.

There are some risks involve in owning a Goldendoodle, so it is important to dog-proof your home.

Let's start with the **kitchen.** This is one of the places where you're likely to find your Goldendoodle often since he or she will constantly be trying to get the food you keep here.

Remember that not all kinds of food are safe for Goldendoodles to eat. Apart from chocolate, which is toxic to all dogs, food that is deadly for you Goldendoodle includes coffee, onions, garlic, grapes, raisins, macadamia nuts, and avocados.

The other things to keep away from your pet are sharp objects (e.g., knives), things he or she can choke on (e.g., twist ties) and things that can suffocate your furry friend (e.g., plastic bags and plastic wrap.) To make sure she doesn't encounter any of these, consider installing a gate or door.

Next is the **living room.** You, your family and guests hang out here, so expect your Goldendoodle to do the same.

If you have a fireplace, install a screen on it to keep the flames out of your pet's reach. This also protects them from the flaming ash.

If you have a regular fireplace, or it isn't automatic, always keep your fire-starter sticks and fireplace rods out of your Goldendoodle's reach as well.

Your Goldendoodle can chew on the cords and wires of the appliances you have in your living room, like an audio system and TV. He or she will get electrocuted if these are plugged in. Tuck them away or cover them to avoid this. You also ought to put away anything valuable or can be a choking hazard (e.g., small toys) when you're away.

If you have a yard, to make sure your Goldendoodle doesn't wander off and get lost, always keep your doors and windows closed, or install a fence or screen.

Your bedroom(s). There are lots of choking hazards here, like coins, buttons, paper clips, rubber bands, batteries, pins, jewelry and hair clips. Make sure you keep these out of sight.

If you use mothballs, put these where you're sure your pet can't reach them. They are toxic.

If you're into crafts, keep any sharp objects you use, like needles, out of sight as well.

If you have a balcony, always keep the door closed so your pet doesn't find his or her way here. She could get stuck in the railings or even jump off and get badly hurt.

The bathroom and the laundry room. Apart from the obvious, like cleansers, detergents, bleach, fabric softeners and your meds, keep your toothbrush, dental floss, and towels out of your Goldendoodle's reach. He or she may be tempted to chew on and swallow or eat these, which could cause your pet to have gastrointestinal problems.

Make sure you didn't leave any of your socks in the laundry room after doing a load, so they don't end up in your pet's tummy either. Always check whether he or she is in the washer or dryer first since these are possible nap spots. So, he or she doesn't become part of your next load of clothes, always keep the doors of your appliances closed.

While it may look harmless, drinking out of the toilet is potentially harmful to your pet. He or she could ingest cleanser residues and get sick, so don't let your pet do it.

If you got a Mini/Toy/Teacup Petite Goldendoodle, never leave sinks and tubs filled with water unattended. He or she could get into these and drown.

The garage and the basement. Not only are there plenty of choking hazards here, like nails, screws, nuts, bolts, small tools and your trinkets that you've put away; there are toxic substances, like pesticides, oils, gasoline, solvents, antifreeze, coolants and de-icing compounds. Keep these high up in a cabinet, always keep this closed and keep your Goldendoodle out.

The outdoors. If you have a garden, know that there are plants that are hazardous to pets. The most common include:

Azaleas and other rhododendron species. Pets that ingest these will suffer from vomiting, diarrhea, and general weakness. If they ate a lot of them, they could die.

Chrysanthemums. While it helps keep pests away, the pyrethrins in chrysanthemums can cause gastrointestinal problems if ingested.

Daffodils and tulips. The bulbs of these flowers contain toxins that can cause a wide range of problems, including drooling, convulsions and cardiac issues.

Hydrangeas. Eating these causes pets to suffer various symptoms: including oral irritation, gastrointestinal distress, and depression.

Yew. The taxine in yew adversely affects the central nervous system that can lead to cardiac failure.

Avoid planting any of these in your garden to keep your Goldendoodle safe and sound. If you have planted any of them, remove them right away.

Apart from certain plants, compost, fertilizers, pesticides, insecticides, cocoa-based mulches, as well as traditional snail and slug bait are toxic for your pet. To keep your Goldendoodle free from harm, stop using these and set up a barrier, or replace them with pet-friendly versions.

If you have a grill and it isn't automatic, always hide the charcoal and lighter fluid.

If you have a pool, spa or pond, keep your Goldendoodle away from the water with some fencing, or keep your pet inside unless accompanied. He or she could drink the water and ingest the toxic chemicals you use to maintain it if it's a pool, or the toxic algae if it's a pond. Either way, he or she could fall in and drown.

How Do I Choose the Right Goldendoodle Puppy or Adult Food?

When you buy your Goldendoodle some dog food, you will be presented with an extensive array to choose from. Each claim to be the best for your new pet, so knowing for sure which is right for your Goldendoodle puppy or adult could be overwhelming. Here is some advice to help you make the best choice.

What Makes a Good Dog Food?

Dog nutrition is a serious business. Knowing what to give to your Goldendoodle will make sure he is healthy all the way.

Good dog food doesn't only contain meat. They also contain vegetables, grains, and fruits. The best dog food contains high-quality versions of these ingredients that are suitable for dogs' digestive systems. This is because dogs are not strictly carnivores, unlike cats. While their diet is mostly made up of meat, domestic dogs also get nutrients from grains, vegetables, and fruits. These aren't fillers. These are an important source of the vitamins, minerals, and fiber that all dogs need.

Dog Nutrition

Needless to say, dog food you ought to choose for your new pet should meet his or her nutritional needs.

While most commercial dog food brands claim to be "specially formulated with at least the minimum nutritional requirements for dogs," not every dog's nutritional needs are the same. They need various nutrients in different amounts in the course of their lives.

Check the Merck Veterinary Manual if you aren't sure about the differences in nutritional requirements among puppies and adult dogs. It lists the recommended nutrients along with the recommended quantities according to age and weight.

How to Read a Dog Food's Label

A good way to find out whether a dog food is good is checking out its label. It should tell you the product's name, the net weight, the name and address of the manufacturer, guaranteed analysis of the dog food, a list of the ingredients, the intended animal species, a statement of the nutritional adequacy and guidelines for feeding.

Look carefully at both the product's name and the list of ingredients. The former will tell you a lot about the dog food. For example: if the product name includes the term 'beef,' then the dog food should be made up of at least 70 percent beef. If it includes 'beef dinner,' 'beef platter' or 'beef entrée,' the dog food will only be 10 percent beef. 'With beef' means it's only three percent beef. 'Beef flavor' means it's less than three percent beef that is just enough to give it a beefy flavor.

The ingredients are more complicated to make out. They won't tell you the quality or where they came from. Some manufacturers split these up to make distribution more equal. For example, different corn types, like ground, flaked and kibbled, can be listed separately. This takes corn down the list, even though the actual content of it is high. Meat is also a tricky ingredient. For instance, the weight of so-called whole meats is made up in large part of water, so the amount of actual meat in there is lower than it seems after processing. On the other hand, while it sounds less appetizing, 'meat meal' actually has more meat than whole meats as they contain no water.

That said, taking a close look at the ingredients is a great way of finding out what is in the dog food. Knowing this is important for dogs with special dietary needs, like allergies. This also ensures your Goldendoodle is getting specific sources of protein, carbohydrates, and fiber if you want.

If a dog food comes with a guaranteed analysis that claims its 'complete and balanced,' you can expect it to be high quality. The Association of American Feed Control Officials (AAFCO) has strict requirements that ensure commercial dog food are indeed complete and balanced. This means they have the minimum amount of all the nutrients dogs need to stay healthy.

Apart from that, the guaranteed analysis also indicates the minimum amount of fat and crude protein, along with the maximum quantities of crude fiber and water, in the dog food. But it doesn't indicate the precise quantities of these components, so there will be variation. If you want to evaluate the product further, check the manufacturer's average nutrient profile. You can also contact the dog food company directly to get more information if you want.

What Is Dry Dog Food?

Dry dog food is the most affordable and widely available dog food type. As it contains approximately 90 percent dry ingredients and only 10 percent water, it does not need to be refrigerated. Being so makes storing it easy. It's made by combining and cooking meat, grains and other ingredients. This process turns the starches into an easily digestible form while getting rid of the toxins and flash-sterilizing the ingredients.

While there are lots of dry dog food you can choose from, the best for your Goldendoodle depends on his or her dietary needs. It should contain ingredients that are appropriate to the stage of his or her life. Consult with a veterinarian or veterinary nutritionist to know for sure.

Wet Dog Food

Wet dog food is canned, has a longer shelf life, is more palatable and contains more meat, along with more textured proteins derived from grains. This makes it more expensive. Once you open one up, you need to keep it in the refrigerator.

Like dry dog food, there is a wide range of wet dog food. Make sure that the ingredients of the one you choose are suitable for your Goldendoodle, and ask or double-check with a veterinarian or veterinary nutritionist.

The Right Dog Food for Your Goldendoodle Puppy

As we've mentioned already, a puppy's nutritional needs are different from an adult dog's, so if you got a puppy, you need to feed furry friend a puppy formula or an 'all life stages' dog food, as well as take his or her size into consideration when making your choice.

The Appropriate Dog Food for Mini/Toy/Teacup/ Petite Goldendoodles and Goldendoodles with a Large-Bred Golden Retriever Parent

Feed your Goldendoodle dog food that contains higher amounts of certain nutrients that promote musculoskeletal health, so he or she avoids having musculoskeletal issues if his or her parent is a large bred Golden Retriever. Due to their size, large dogs are more prone to musculoskeletal problems than small dogs.

If he or she is a Mini/Toy/Teacup/Petite Goldendoodle, make sure the size of her kibble is just right that he or she doesn't choke on them.

If your Goldendoodle has special dietary needs (e.g., allergies or a sensitive stomach), ask a veterinarian about what type of dog food will be suitable for her condition. It can be complicated to feed your pet yourself properly since professional knowledge and experience is needed.

What Are the Essential Goldendoodle Gear?

An adjustable nylon collar with a plastic clasp. 10" to 14" is a good fit for standard or medium Goldendoodle puppies, and 8" to 12" for Mini/Toy/Teacup/Petite Goldendoodle puppies.

- **I.D. tag**
- **At least 15 ft. (4.6 m) or longer (up to 50 ft. (15 m) training leash(es)**

- **6 ft. (1.8 m) leash**
- **Paper towels** to clean up after your Goldendoodle puppy or adult.
- **Pooper scooper and bags**
- **A place to sleep,** like a basket or crate.
- **Old towels or blanket** to serve as bedding.
- **Food and water bowls.** Buy either stainless steel or ceramic, so it lasts long
- **Storage bin** if you choose dry dog food.
- **Cotton balls** for cleaning out the ears.
- **Nail file** to file down the nails when they get too long.
- **Baby gate(s)** to keep your Goldendoodle out of potentially hazardous places, like the kitchen. Avoid the ones with horizontal bars and large spaces in between the bars. He or she can climb up the horizontal bars. If he or she is small, she can slip through if the spaces are large.

Stain/odor neutralizer

- **Bitter Apple spray.** The bitter taste will discourage your pet from biting, gnawing and licking
- **Hydrogen peroxide** to induce vomiting, if needed, like if he or she accidentally swallows something he or she shouldn't have.
- **Wire crate** for crate training
- **Double-door, folding crate with a divider.** If you got a Standard Goldendoodle, he or she would need a crate that is at least a 42" (1.07 m). If you have a Mini/Toy/Teacup/

Petite Goldendoodle, he or she would be fine with a 36" (0.9 m) crate.

- **Travel crate.** If you get a puppy, you will need this until he or she is big enough to wear a harness.

Training treats. Soft, tiny treats (e.g., pieces of cheese or hot dogs) are most effective.

Grooming Supplies

- Shampoo
- Conditioner/Grooming spray
- Medium-tooth comb
- Pin/slicker brush
- Ear wash solution
- Toothbrush kit
- Pliers-style nail clippers with a nail guard
- A pair or blunt, curved scissors
- Blood-stop powder

What Are Great Goldendoodle Gifts?

Nothing can make your new furry pal feel welcome and loved like gifts. Here are some that we're sure he or she will like.

- **Puppy biscuits.** They should be high in protein, have a healthy amount of fat, contain little or no byproducts and unnatural additives, like artificial colors.

- **Traditional toys,** like balls, stuffed dog toys, and rope toys. These will provide your Goldendoodle with lots of entertainment, help prevent them from gnawing on your stuff and make them so much more adorable.

- **Auto-refilling dog bowl.** Just like its name describes, this bowl can refill itself. You can attach it to a wall or other outdoor surface, as well as your garden hose.

- **Dog peek window.** Just the right shape and size for your new pet, you can install this spherical window into any wooden fence for fun-filled snooping.

- **Hyper dog ball launcher.** Able to launch a tennis ball as far as 200 ft., you will never have to worry about your dog outlasting you at fetch.

CHAPTER 6

Taking Your Goldendoodle Home: What Is the Best Way to Do It?

A s much as you want to take your Goldendoodle home as soon as possible to start spending time with your pet, you need to hold your horses to be able to go about it the right way.

It's not as simple as coaxing your furry friend into your car, making your way back home as fast yet as safely as you can, and carrying or guiding your new furry pal into the house.

There are several things you need to do so that the trip and your first day together turns out well.

This chapter will teach you all about them, from how to keep your Goldendoodle secure and snug throughout the ride, to how to make his or her first day and night with you turn out well.

A gift for you

Enjoy Hope this book is helpful! I am so excited (and jealous)! Happy BD! From Love and miss you! Karin

Goldendoodle at the park! There is nothing more joyful than bringing your pet to the park the moment you get one.

The Trip Back: How Do I Keep My Goldendoodle as Safe and Comfortable as Possible?

To begin with, **take some bottled water and a bowl so your Goldendoodle can drink during the ride.**

Dogs need a readily available source of water, especially on a long trip, so make sure you have some to drink on hand for your new pet when he or she needs to, and there isn't any store nearby.

A bowl lets you avoid making a mess since it will be much harder to make your Goldendoodle drink right from the bottle. This means you have to make a stop each time he or she needs a drink, but it will be well worth it since you're much less likely to have an accident.

That said, **don't feed your Goldendoodle while driving.** Feed your pet at a rest stop instead. If your Goldendoodle doesn't have motion sickness, give your dog enough time to digest before getting back on the road. Half an hour will be more than enough.

Avoid bringing your Goldendoodle any toys. While you would think it's a good idea since it will keep your furry friend preoccupied, it's better for both of you to just keep your pet relaxed throughout the ride yourself instead. If you suddenly hit a bump or pothole, or he or she gets too excited, your Goldendoodle could accidently swallow the toys and choke on them.

Remember to take your Goldendoodle's collar, ID tag, and leash with you. The collar and ID prove he or she is your pet in case you get pulled over and questioned. The leash helps you guide your Goodendoodle and maintain control.

Make sure the ID tag has your phone number. If you're adopting an adult Goldendoodle and he or she is microchipped, don't forget to register your contact information with the chip's company if the shelter or rescue group did not.

If you feel it will be difficult for you to hoist your pet into your car, get a ramp or steps so he or she can climb into your car with little or no trouble.

Decide where to put your Goldendoodle's bed, food and water bowls, crate, food, treats and supplies (i.e., toys, treats, pooper scooper and plastic bags, grooming tools, etc.). Preparing in advance lets you avoid the confusion of having to put everything in order when you bring your Goldendoodle home while keeping a close eye on your pet. Place his or her bowls in a safe, out-of-the-way area of the house so you, your family and guests don't accidently step on these or kick them.

Take a friend or family member with you. You can leave your Goldendoodle with them while you buy some food or use a toilet and not worry that something might happen to your new pet, making the trip easier and safer.

When you pick up your Goldendoodle, ask what kind of dog food he or she was fed and when. Suddenly changing these can cause your furry friend to have gastric problems, so feed your Goldendoodle the same dog food at the same time for at least the first few days. If you switch to a different brand or kind, do so gradually for about a week by feeding them one part of the new dog food and three parts of the old one, then 50/50, then one part of the old with three parts of the new.

Keep your Goldendoodle in a solid crate. You shouldn't let your Goldendoodle roam freely in your car since this increases your risk of having an accident. To ensure both of your safety, keep your pet in a crate instead, and make sure you secure the crate down using a seat belt or something similar. This is the safest way for you to travel in a car together. While there are restraints, like seat belts, for dogs that can prevent them from moving about a car unnecessarily, none has been proven to protect them in a crash.

To make sure your new pet is protected, the crate should be made of sturdy materials, like aluminum or plastic reinforced with fiberglass; it's the right size for your pooch; its safety is certified; it's been crash-tested, and it allows for adequate air circulation.

If you live in a place where the climate is colder or hotter than most, go far a crate with good insulation to ensure your Goldendoodle stays comfortable.

To make the trip much safer, you can consider getting a crate with air bags. These will keep your pooch safe and sound if you suddenly break hard, you have to make an emergency break or— God forbid! —you have an accident.

A good way to determine whether a crate for dogs is high quality is whether it's made by a brand that adheres to strict quality guidelines. Reputable brands offer at least a two-year warranty.

Place your Goldendoodle in the backseat. While it may be more entertaining for your new pet to let your furry friend sit in front with you, it's safer to keep them in the back. Otherwise, if your airbags deploy, even if you kept your pet in a crate, get hurting is a possibility.

Take breaks if you think your trip will take several hours. Traveling with a dog is like traveling with a child. You need to make a stop every two or three hours so he or she can get out, stretch his or her legs and do his or her business. You ought not to keep going even if you could. While you can push yourself to drive for hours on end to get back home sooner, your

Goldendoodle has different needs. Besides, staying on the road for too long is bad for you. Enjoy the time you will be able to spend with your pooch instead.

That said, **don't take any unnecessary side trips.** It will be safer for both of you to bring your pet straight home.

Avoid having guests over. While throwing your Goldendoodle, a welcoming party could be loads of fun, being exposed to a lot of enthusiastic strangers can overwhelm your dog, causing them to misbehave or even snap. Keep your dogs first day quiet and simple instead.

Introducing Your Goldendoodle to His or Her New Home: How Do I Go About It?

Once you get back home, **let your Goldendoodle sniff around your yard or outside on a leash before taking your furry friend inside your home.** Dogs learn about things best through their keen sense of smell, so let your Goldendoodle do his or her thing to get to know his or her new environment.

Once he or she is done, **let your Goldendoodle meet your family outside, one at a time.** Keep everybody calm and relaxed, so your Goldendoodle doesn't get overwhelmed, nervous, startled, frightened or agitated. Tell your family to avoid kissing, hugging, picking up, staring at, or patting your furry friend on the head. These can be alarming for some dogs. Let him, or her be the one to approach and set the pace and tone of the introduction. To help new dog warm up to them, your family can offer them a treat.

If you have another dog or dogs, introduce your Goldendoodle to him, her or them outside as well. Just like with your family, get them to know each other one at a time. Let them take as much time as they need. Keep their leashes loose to make them as comfortable as possible. There ought not to be any food or toys around. These can excite them. Watch them carefully to avoid any accidents. Leave them alone only if you're sure it's safe.

If you have a cat or cats, secure him, her or them until you find out what your Goldendoodle will do when he or she sees them. Prevent your pet from chasing them by keeping them separated. To make sure nothing bad happens, give your cat or cat escape routes. When they do meet, keep your pets' initial encounter as brief as possible, and watch them closely the whole time.

Once everybody has been formally introduced, **take your Goldendoodle into your house on a leash and give them a tour.** Continue keeping your dog calm and relaxed to stop any grabbing and gnawing of your stuff. If your furry friend persists, make a 'leave-it' gesture and offer a toy, instead, to keep your new dog preoccupied.

Start training your Goldendoodle. The first thing you need to do is come up with a list of verbal and nonverbal commands that you and your family can use. Not only will this let you avoid any confusion, but your new pet will also learn faster.

Take your Goldendoodle to the place where you've chosen to let him, or her do his or her business and give a reward him of a treat for going there. This ensures he or she learns where to go by themselves.

Make sure your Goldendoodle gets sufficient quiet time. This prevents the pet from getting overwhelmed and exhausted. It's best to let him, or her decide when, where and how much time she needs, so pay close attention, and follow his or her lead.

Come up with a basic daily structure and routine that include some rules for your Goldendoodle. This will work out best if you let your family help you. Not only will you know what to do; since everybody is allowed to give their input, the rules are more likely to be followed. Also set the boundaries, including whether he or she will be allowed on the couch, and if there are rooms that need to be off-limits.

Make sure you know what your chores are. Who will be the one to walk your new pet first thing in the morning? Who will feed your furry buddy in the evening? To avoid any confusion, set the schedule for walks, feeding, doing his or her business, training and playing. It's better to divide the responsibilities, so everybody gets to take care of your new pet. This ensures everybody bonds with your Goldendoodle.

More importantly, your pooch will enjoy the comfort of consistency. Aside from knowing what is expected of your puppy, they can count on you, day in and day out. Your puppy will know when exactly he or she will be fed, walked, bathed, groomed, let out to do bathroom business and allowed to play. Having a routine lets your furry pet settle in easily and quickly.

Consult with a trusted veterinarian or veterinary nutritionist about what the recommended kind and amount of dog food is

best for your Goldendoodle based on his or her health, size, age and level of activity.

Your Goldendoodle's First Night: How Do I Help My Puppy Adjust?

If you're getting a puppy, expect him, or her to feel alone and nervous or even scared on the first night, making her restless and whine as loudly as he or she can all night and even until dawn.

Don't keep your puppy in the basement, garage or in a cage to keep the noise down and prevent the scratching at the doors and escaping. According to most veterinarians, this could cause your pooch to have behavioral problems as he or she grows up, making it hard—if not impossible—to raise, train and take care of them properly.

Instead of keeping your dog away from you, make a place where he or she can hang out, rest and sleep comfortably and not feel isolated.

While you'd be fine with keeping your dog or puppy on a blanket on the floor in your bedroom for the first night, this is not safe for both of you since he or she has not yet been house-trained. Instead, keep your pet in a crate, keep the crate in your bedroom, or right outside, and keep the door open. Aside from he or she can calm down and relax knowing you're just nearby, you can hear your Goldendoodle easily if he or she needs to go out and do his or her business.

Very young pups have limited bladder capacity, making them unable to hold it in the whole night, so you will need to take your puppy outside so he or she can relieve him- or herself. Apart from keeping the house clean, until he or she grows, making it a habit of walking before going to bed, even if it's just to and from the yard, will tire your pet out, letting your dog fall asleep more easily and sleep more soundly, ensuring you get a good night's sleep.

To help your dog calm down and relax, give your puppy a toy, like a stuffed plushy, before leaving your new puppy for the night and going to bed. It can make your little one comfortable enough to settle down.

Avoid making a fuss out of leaving when you go so your puppy won't get more agitated.

CHAPTER 7

Making Your Goldendoodle Part of Your Life: What Is the Right Way?

Your new pet Goldendoodle isn't the only one that needs to adapt to ensure you can start a great new life together. You'll also have to adjust. You'll learn all about these in this chapter, from how to take care of a Goldendoodle puppy, to how to properly settle in with your new pet, whether he or she is a growing Goldendoodle or a Goldendoodle adult. You'll also learn the correct way to discipline a Goldendoodle here.

Raising Goldendoodles is no easy task. Doing it the right way will give you lots of joy.

Raising a Goldendoodle: How Do I Raise Mine Properly?

If you got yourself a Goldendoodle puppy, raising him, or her properly will depend on how well you crate train your puppy.

Crate training is a way of teaching a pet to accept a crate as a place where he or she can stay or rest without worrying that something bad might happen to your precious new pet.

You might think that training your Goldendoodle to be kept in a crate willingly is cruel, and it will be better to let your pet sleep in your bed. But it's actually okay- and good in the long term!

In fact, a crate wouldn't be an unusual environment for puppies in general. It would be instinctive for them to find and live in a small, hiding place-like spot since they have a little wolf in them.

Dogs are believed to have originated from gray wolves. This is why dogs nap under a table or chair, similar to how a gray wolf would sleep in a hole or cave.

A crate is similar to these, so your puppy would be fine staying in one as long as he or she hasn't had a bad experience of being confined.

To make the create really appeal to his or her den-dwelling instinct, you could drape some fabric over the back half that will cover it, like a blanket, to simulate a dark, den-like environment that he or she will be drawn to, ensuring he or she will make it his or her spot.

More important than giving your pet its own spot at home that will suit them, crate training lets you train your puppy faster in a way that is good for his or her health. For instance, he or she will learn how to 'hold it in.' It's puppies' nature not to mess up their dens.

That said, as we've mentioned already, puppies' bladder capacity is limited, so don't expect your Goldendoodle to keep his or her spot spotless if you don't take yet puppy out for frequent and consistent potty trips.

Apart from holding it in, your puppy will learn not to wander around the house at night, which could result in an accident, like get into the trash or fight with your other pets.

To make sure crate training your puppy turns out to be a success, keep it positive. Avoid using it as punishment. For instance, never force your dog to go into or out of the crate.

If you force your puppy into or out of the crate, he or she will develop a dislike for it—making it unlikely if not impossible to train your dog to make the crate its own spot.

Everything about crate training your puppy needs to be positive from his or her viewpoint to make it work. If you make your dog go into and stay in the crate even when they don't want to, or you pull, yank or shake the puppy out, makes it feel unsafe just being around the crate, defeating the purpose of the dog's training.

The goal is to train your puppy to go into or out of the crate on their own when you ask him. For encouragement, you can put treats, like toys, in the crate. Keep doing so even after your dog gets used to the crate to ensure your dog goes through the entire duration of crate training.

Leaving your puppy in the crate for a few hours at first will do just fine. Avoid leaving your pet there for more than eight hours. She could become restless, nervous or agitated.

Some dogs take a long time to learn how to settle down at night. There are those that take years, so be patient.

Adjusting to a Goldendoodle Puppy, Growing Goldendoodle, and Full Grown Goldendoodle

Living in a new home is a major change in your Goldendoodle's life, whether he or she is a puppy, is still growing or is an adult dog.

Again, he or she will need to make a lot of adjustments, like get to know you, your family or your other pets; learn your communication style, and get used to his or her new environment.

This can be a lot to take in at first, so he or she could get stressed out and misbehave, like have housetraining accidents, avoid everyone, bark excessively or try to escape. He or she could also lose his or her appetite or suffer from an upset stomach.

The different environment, with different smells, noises and people or animals that treat it differently. All these new things coupled with your expectations of this pet will stress the pet, so you need to be patient enough to give your Goldendoodle as much time as is needed to adjust to their new life.

Imagine getting air-dropped into a foreign country where
everything is different—you don't know anybody, the rules
for proper behavior are peculiar and you can't speak the local
language. You would surely be confused—if not overwhelmed.
Living with you now might not be as extreme as this scenario for
your Goldendoodle, but it could be close.

If you adopted a Goldendoodle, the scenario could be different,
but he or she could still feel stressed about it. He or she may see
you, your family or your other pets as another stopover, another
point in his or her life where she needs to wait and not get too
close to anybody so it can move on unscathed.

He or she may have been through a difficult journey. He or she
may have been neglected or homeless before getting rescued. He
or she may have gone through various shelters, people and other
animals before you found and discovered him, so your pet might
not know right away that your home is their new true home.

It's best you give your Goldendoodle a lot of space for the first
few days. As much as you want to, avoid doing anything too
strenuous the first few days. Also, don't make demand on your
new dog either.

If you have a growing or adult Goldendoodle, use a crate or
kennel to keep a close eye on your pet and prevent any bad
behavior. You can also consider tying your pet to a piece of
furniture and staying close-by, or tie your fluffy pet to your waist.

Walk your pet to ensure that it gets enough exercise. This is the
best form of exercise for your puppy at first as they might not
want to play for the first few days.

Among the causes of your Goldendoodle's stress is not knowing what to expect from the new environment. So, another thing you can do to get the adjustment process done quicker is to create a routine for your pet, including how many times to feed and exercise your Goldendoodle each day, when to put your dog to sleep or go out. Such consistency creates a sense of security that will enable faster adjustment.

Once your dog is beginning to adjust, start letting your Goldendoodle roam freely for short periods. If you feel that you still need to guide it, allow your pet to drag its leash. If your pet behaves, gradually increase the free time. This includes periods that he or she is unattended, like when you get the mail. Keep giving Goldendoodle more free time until you can leave your puppy alone alone.

Keep in mind that getting through the adjustment period can take longer and be harder than you think. There are various dog temperaments, including calm, social, confident, willful and dominant. Some temperaments are much harder to deal with than others.

If your Goldendoodle has behavioral issues, ask your family to help you. You can, for example, attend an obedience class (or a few) where you can bond with your new pet and figure out how to manage his or her behavioral problems. The sooner you do, the sooner you can deal with them.

Goldendoodle: What Are the Appropriate Things to Do?

If you got a Goldendoodle puppy, you need to let him, or her socialize.

It's crucial for your pup's well-being to socialize during her first three months of his or her life, and before he or she reaches 14 to 16 weeks. This is the time when his or her sociability is stronger than his or her fear. His or her brain is wide open to accept new things and experiences. Whatever they are, they will dictate her character, temperament, and behavior for the rest of his or her life.

Puppies that aren't allowed to socialize during their first three months are at great risk of developing behavioral issues, like fearfulness, avoidance, and aggression. They grow up into problematic dogs that end up in shelters.

To properly socialize your puppy, you need to expose it to as many people, animals, and environments as possible. But make sure your furry pet doesn't get overwhelmed. This can cause fear and your Goldendoodle may withdraw, preventing learning socialization skills.

Letting your puppy socialize isn't just putting your puppy in the car for a ride, or walking it down the street, or to the park. Having other pets around isn't proper socializing either. This requires:

- Being handled since birth
- Learning to accept having all his or her body parts touched

- Being exposed to various stimuli, like playing with various toys and games on different surfaces
- Being encouraged to explore their environment
- Being exposed to as many people, other animals, environments and situations as possible

To ensure your puppy socializes properly, enroll it in classes and playgroups for puppies; let him, or her interact with other people and pets; expose your pupply to different smells, sights, and sounds; and handle her routinely, like bathing and grooming her regularly.

If you have another pet or pets, do your homework and consult a specialist in animal behavior before bringing your Goldendoodle puppy home to ensure there won't be any trouble between your puppy and your other pets when they meet.

Disciplining Your Goldendoodle: What Are the Things I Need to Do and Ought Not to Do?

It's always better to correct your Goldendoodle than punish them for a mistake.

A correction is an expression of disapproval when the mistake is being made or has been made. Punishment is anything you do after which can be more severe.

Say your Goldendoodle jumped through a screen. Punishing does nothing but confuse your puppy, damaging the trust between you two, and preventing your pet from learning what your puppy ought to have learned.

Dogs' sense of logic is different from humans. Unlike us, they don't plan or reason out situations. For example, your Goldendoodle could relate that you're angry after he or she jumped through the screen. But he or she won't figure out that if he or she didn't jump through the screen in the first place, you wouldn't be angry. All he or she knows is that you'll get mad after he or she makes a mistake.

Whatever a dog is doing, at the moment you punish them, is what they will think is bad. For instance, if the dog is lying on his or her owner's bed when the owner gets angry, the dog will think lying on the bed is what the owner is mad about. In the case of your Goldendoodle jumping through the screen, the dog will understand that you're angry after he or she made a mistake, but he or she will not understand why it's wrong or make the connection between it and the punishment. Unless you catch your dog in the act of jumping through the screen, your dog will keep jumping through showing you that they do not know that what he or she is doing is bad. Without on the mark punishment, your pet will always miss the reasoning behind it, defeating the purpose of the punishment.

CHAPTER 8

Caring for Your Goldendoodle: How Do I Do It Correctly?

Inasmuch as it's rewarding and a lot of fun, having a Goldendoodle as a pet is a big responsibility.

Each dog is unique, having complicated needs that their owners need to understand to be able to take care of them. These include diet, grooming, exercise and preventive care.

To ensure you're able to care for your Goldendoodle as best as you can, this chapter teaches how to make sure your pooch eats the right kinds of food, the right way to groom your pet, how to keep your pet fit, and how to reduce your pet's risk of getting sick.

A picture of a healthy Goldendoodle. As an owner,
it is important to care for your pet.

Keeping Your Goldendoodle's Diet Balanced: How Do I Make Sure My Fur Baby Always Eats Healthy Food?

Ensuring your Goldendoodle's diet remains balanced is necessary for optimum health. Doing so enables consumption of all the nutrients needed by your dog to stay healthy.

Nutrients are the substances in food that your pet needs to live and grow. The essentials are proteins, carbohydrates, fiber, vitamins, minerals, and fat.

Proteins refer to the basic building blocks of cells, which you and your Goldendoodle are made up of. Needless to say, they are essential for all the processes that naturally go on in the bodies of living things, including growth and maintenance.

Sources of protein include chicken, beef, fish and eggs. Vegetables, cereals, and soy are also sources of protein, but they are considered incomplete proteins.

Avoid giving your Goldendoodle raw eggs. Raw egg white has an 'antivitamin' called avidin that prevents dogs from metabolizing fats, glucose, amino acids, and energy.

Carbohydrates are natural substances that provide energy, are crucial to keeping the intestines healthy, and are needed for reproduction. Take for example fibers. These carbohydrates can help your Goldendoodle manage chronic diarrhea. Good sources of fiber include beet pulp, grains, like corn, wheat and rice, and wheat middling.

Veterinarians and veterinary nutritionists advise against feeding dog food that is high in fiber to young and growing dogs as well as those with a high-energy requirement.

Vitamins are organic substances that your Goldendoodle needs for nourishment but only in small amounts.

Unless you're told by a veterinarian, avoid giving your pet a vitamin supplement. Otherwise, he or she could suffer over supplementation or hypervitaminosis, which is basically poisoning due to consuming too many vitamins. For example, excess vitamin A can cause bone-dry skin, brittle bones, as well as bone and joint pain.

Minerals refer to the substances that your Goldendoodle needs to make up his or her bones and teeth, to keep the fluids in his or her body balanced and to enable his or her body to keep functioning properly. He or she can't make these him- or herself, so he or she must be provided with these in his or her diet to stay healthy.

While most people avoid them, fats are quite important to your Goldendoodle's health. They give the pet more than twice the energy he or she gets from proteins and carbohydrates. They are an essential part of cells. They are needed to produce certain hormones. Your pet needs them to absorb and use certain vitamins. They protect the internal organs. They provide insulation. Having a deficiency in essential fatty acids, like linoleic acid, leads to stunted growth or worsening of existing skin problems.

Goldendoodle Grooming: How Do I Keep My Golden Doodle Dog Looking Good?

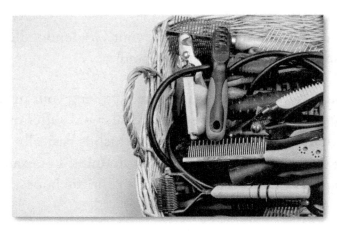

An assortment of grooming tools for your Goldendoodle.

98

Whether it's curly, wavy, shaggy or straight, your Goldendoodle's coat needs regular maintenance to stay stunning. You could take your Goldendoodle to a groomer for some grooming, but it will be more convenient—and fun—if you do it yourself.

The first thing to keep in mind is, always detangle your Goldendoodle's coat before bathing. Shampooing a tangled coat will worsen the knots of fur, hurting your furry pet.

Next, pluck out your Goldendoodle's ears. Because of having Poodle genes, fur grows inside the dog's ear canals. The fur traps bacteria along with moisture, increasing your pet's risk of having an ear infection.

To pluck out your Goldendoodle's ears, firmly take hold of the fur using your thumb and pointer finger and then pull it out as quickly as you can. Pulling out large sections of it is hard and painful, so pull out the fur little by little instead.

Once you've removed all the fur, insert some dry cotton balls into both the ear canals and then gently fold down the outer ear flaps to keep the water out during the bath. Immediately take out the cotton balls afterward.

Comb your Goldendoodle's coat with a metal pin brush until it glides through your dog's fur. Hold it firmly and only brush in one direction to avoid making knots. If it gets stuck, go back and carefully tease out the knot. Start at the end of the strands and move toward your pet's skin for the desired result.

To wring out excess moisture from your Goldendoodle's coat and apply conditioner, use your fingers and start at the top of its body, work your way down to his or her paws and rinse thoroughly.

When drying your Goldendoodle's coat with a towel, pat individual sections of the coat firmly instead of rubbing or ruffling it. Doing so can create knots.

When blow-drying your Goldendoodle's fur, brush only in the direction that it grows and avoid moving it with your hands to avoid creating knots.

Shave your Goldendoodle's belly, genital region, and anus. The fur on his or her belly and around the genitals and anus act like a sponge for bacteria, increasing risk of getting an infection, so shave these areas smooth with electric clippers. Also, shave the fur an inch below his or her ear canals to ensure proper air flow through his or her ears.

Exercising Your Goldendoodle: How Do I Help My Goldendoodle Stay Fit?

Just like you, your Goldendoodle needs regular exercise to stay healthy.

Properly exercising your dog doesn't mean just letting your dog out to play in the yard once a day. Dogs generally need at least 30 minutes of vigorous exercise each day. Depending on their medical history and age, some need more.

Ensuring your Goldendoodle gets the right amount of exercise will do wonders for your fluffy pet. Not only will it look great, but your dog will also feel better.

To achieve or maintain your Goldendoodle's ideal weight, you need to determine your dog's daily calorie requirement. This is based on body weight, activity level and age.

For example, the more active your dog is, the more you can feed them. If you exercise your dog more on the weekends, you can feed them more than you do on the weekdays since the additional workout prevents your pet from gaining weight even when eating more.

That said, you need to accurately measure how much you feed your Goldendoodle to make sure you keep within its daily range. An easy way to do this is with a measuring cup. If you want to go high tech, or you don't have anyone who can take care of your Goldendoodle for you when you're away, you can use a device, like a smart pet feeder.

Be careful with the treats and feeding your Goldendoodle from the table. Your dog could overeat and become overweight if you aren't careful. If you can't help giving your fur baby treats, feed it small treats, or break up regular-size treats into smaller pieces before feeding these to your pet instead. Thus, the dog will still get the reward but only a fraction of the calories normally contained, preventing weight gain.

Preventive Care and Maintenance for Your Goldendoodle's Health: How Do I Ensure My Goldendoodle Does Not Get Sick?

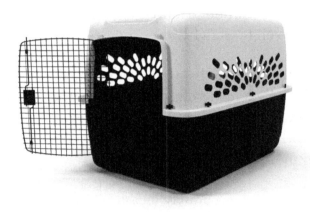

A cage is the perfect protection for a Goldendoodle, especially in traveling.

Common dog ailments typically originate from their stomachs. The cause could be anything that irritates their tummies or prevents the contents from moving along naturally. The causes for dogs to have an upset stomach include an infection and eating or swallowing things they shouldn't have, like toys, socks, poisonous plants, and thrash.

If your Goldendoodle has a mild tummy ache:

• Avoid feeding your pet for at least 24 hours

• Afterward, slowly feed your pet in small quantities.

• Provide your pet with some water to drink.

- If your pet vomits, give it a few tablespoons of water each hour, or offer it some ice cubes every couple of hours instead, and hold out on giving your pet food for another 10 hours. This prevents it from drinking too much water that can upset the pet's stomach more but still help it stop vomiting.

- Once your pet stops vomiting, feed it 2-3 teaspoons of bland food, like plain chicken or rice, each hour.

- Once your dog is well again, you can resume feeding your pet, as usual, the next day.

- If he or she is still sick (i.e., he or she can't keep water down; there's blood or unusual material in his or her vomit; or is uncomfortable, lethargic or bloated), take your pet to a veterinarian as soon as possible.

Another common ailment among dogs is **fleas** and **dandruff.** To ensure your Goldendoodle avoids having these:

- Give your pet a bath every month or two. More will dry out his or her skin.

- Avoid using any shampoo and conditioner that contain chemicals. Use a natural shampoo made specifically for pets or a castile soap instead.

- Make sure you shampoo your Goldendoodle's whole body and reach his or her skin. Let it sit for five minutes before rinsing. Do so gently. Use a spray attachment to make it as easy as possible. Use lukewarm water to ensure your pet stays comfortable.

- To not only prevent fleas from getting into your Goldendoodle's coat but also make the coat shine, you can pour and massage or spray some diluted apple cider vinegar into the coat. Make sure you avoid your pet's eyes. Pat your dog down with a towel until it is just damp and let the rest of the solution dry out naturally.

Aside from fleas and dandruff, itching is also common among dogs. If your Goldendoodle suffers from this:

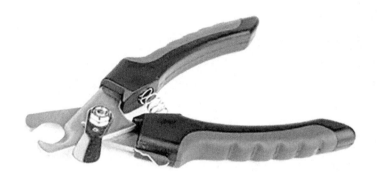

A nail clipper is a must-have if you own a Goldendoodle.

- Clip away the fur on the inflamed area(s)
- Bathe your Goldendoodle with a mild, organic soap for pets.
- Once your pet is dry, wash the affected area(s) with some black or green tea that has steeped for at least 10 minutes and then cooled. The tannic acid in tea dries out the skin, reducing the oozing caused by the inflammation. **Make sure your dog doesn't drink any of the tea. Tea can be toxic for dogs.**
- Apply some vitamin E oil or aloe vera gel onto the affected area two or three times a day.
- Depending on your Goldendoodle's size, give it:

- 1/2 a teaspoon to two tablespoons of nutritional yeast. This will provide your dog with some more protein and B vitamins.

- 1/4 teaspoon to one tablespoon of granular lecithin. This will help your Goldendoodle digest fats, improving its coat.

- Two to three drops to a full dropper of cod-liver oil. This supplies your dog with vitamins A and D, both of which keep your Goldendoodle's skin supple.

- One teaspoon to two tablespoons of cold-pressed, unsaturated vegetable oil for dogs. This provides your dog with some more essential fatty acids.

- One or two drops of a pricked vitamin E capsule or some similar formula for pets. Adding any of these to one of your Goldendoodle's daily meals keeps her skin healthy.

- 15 to 20 mg of chelated zinc per day. This lets your pet avoid having a zinc deficiency, which is a cause of itchy skin.

CHAPTER 9

Goldendoodle Training for Beginners or Nonprofessionals: How Do I Do It Effectively?

Your Goldendoodle needs to learn how to behave properly around you, your family or your other pets so you can live well together.

The rules for proper behavior among dogs are different from those among people, so you need to help your pooch learn them by training it.

This chapter provides you with great tips to successfully teach your new pet easy tricks, mid-level tricks and hard tricks. You'll also learn about the training gear you'll need and the things to consider when choosing here.

An assortment of balls that Goldendoodle loves to play with.

Easy Tricks: How Do I Start?

Choose your Goldendoodle's name carefully. You might not think to start out by doing so, but you ought to. How much thought you give it affects how well training your Goldendoodle turns out.

For example: Giving your Goldendoodle a short name with a strong ending, like Jack or Ginger, makes training him or her easier. It's easy for you to pronounce and your pooch will hear it clearly as long as you emphasize the ending properly.

If you got an adult Goldendoodle, it's okay to change his or her name if he or she was already given one. His or her old name could be long or difficult to pronounce, making using it a pain.

If your pet came from a bad situation, giving it a new name helps them leave the bad experience behind, ensuring a fresh start with you.

Generally, dogs adapt well to new people, animals, environments and situations, so don't worry too much about the name you'll give your Goldendoodle. If you use it consistently, it will respond to it.

Aside from making it short and have a distinct-sounding ending, you ought to give your Goldendoodle a positive-sounding name. Your dog will associate it with nice things, ensuring good response to it.

Train your Goldendoodle to come when you call it. This is the command your pooch needs to learn to obey first. It reinforces the owner-pet relationship between the two of you, making it easier to train your dog.

To make sure it works, always use the name you've given your pet and mix up the times you do by calling them when they are busy.

The more you train your dog to come during his infancy and into maturity, the more ingrained to obey it will be.

Deal with your Goldendoodle jumping up and down during training properly. While it's adorable, avoid encouraging this excited behavior. It makes properly training difficult.

Scolding or punishing your dog will develop a dislike for or fear of training, so it's best to ignore the behavior when it starts acting up and wait for your pet to settle down before getting back to training instead.

Reward your Goldendoodle when it does well. Praising him or her, giving your pet a treat, or letting them play a little is positive reinforcement that encourages and keeps your pet doing well in training, increasing your chances of success.

If you have a play biter, discourage your puppy from being so by pretending to get hurt each time your pet play-bites or gnaws at you.

As we've discussed already, scolding and punishment aren't effective on dogs because they process these differently from the way people normally do.

By pretending to get hurt when your Goldendoodle play-bites or gnaws at you instead, your pet will be so surprised that it will stop immediately.

If this doesn't work, distract them by giving him or her a toy.

If your Goldendoodle still keeps at it, stop the behavior and ignore the dog for a while.

Always end your Goldendoodle's training sessions on a positive note. Giving your furry friend a lot of encouragement, praise, a treat, some enthusiastic petting, or letting your pet play for a few minutes encourages them to keep doing his or her best.

Be consistent. For example, always make your Goldendoodle come to you the same way you first taught it to come to you. Repetition ensures what you're teaching sticks. Remember, dogs tend to forget something just minutes after doing it.

Mid-Level Tricks: What Are the Things to Consider?

Toilet training is among the harder but necessary things for your Goldendoodle to learn. Apart from being as patient as possible, use the proper training methods, because they work.

- **If you have a puppy,** start when he or she is 3-4 months. If you start earlier, your furry friend won't have enough bowel and bladder control to pull it off. Any later will make getting it done harder and longer.

- **Begin training your Goldendoodle by confining it in one spot of the house,** like one of your rooms, the length of his or her leash when it's tied, or the pet's crate. This teaches her that his or her 'business' should be done outside. As your pet learns, gradually give it more space to roam until you're sure it will do its business outside even if you allow it to roam freely.

- **Stay outside with your Goldendoodle while your pet is doing his or her business.** This shows that you are toilet training your pet, not just letting it go outside. This also prevents the pet from wandering off and getting lost if it is not yet house-trained.

- **Always take your Goldendoodle to the same spot.** Your fluffy friend will recognize their scent left there previously, indicating that it's their own person spot to do business, encouraging them to do business faster because they are secure in their own spot.

- **Give your Goldendoodle lots of opportunities to do its business each day.** First thing in the morning, every 30 minutes to 1 hour throughout the day, after your dog finishes a meal, and after taking a nap will do just fine.

- **Reward your Goldendoodle for doing well.** As we've mentioned already, positive reinforcement encourages your dog to learn what you're teaching her.

Hard Tricks: How Do I Make Them as Easy as Possible?

Obedience training is harder than teaching your Goldendoodle to come to you and do its business outside, but it's necessary to ensure that there will be as less trouble between you as possible.

Here are the basic commands your Goldendoodle needs to learn to respond to, aside from 'come' to be trained in obedience.

- **Sit.** This helps you keep control of your Goldendoodle in virtually any situation.
- **Heel.** This teaches your Goldendoodle to remain close to you while walking, with or without a leash, which makes being out and about easier and much more fun for both of you.
- **Drop.** This teaches your Goldendoodle to immediately let go of whatever it is holding in his or her mouth. This is particularly useful since it could save his or her life if he or she picks up and tries to eat or swallow something harmful.
- **Stay.** This teaches your Goldendoodle to keep still and calm in one place, which ensures good behavior in the company of others or when you must leave them unsupervised for a bit.

As always, reward your Goldendoodle for doing well to make sure it keeps at it.

Goldendoodle Training Gear: How Do I Pick Out the Best?

You need several things to train your Goldendoodle properly. These are a collar or a harness, a leash and a crate.

Both a collar and a harness connect you and your Goldendoodle together with a leash, can hold a tag that has important information about your pet, have a role in training.

But if your Goldendoodle has a throat disease, a harness will be safer. Originally designed to wrap around a dog's upper body to let it pull heavy loads, a harness poses virtually no risk of exacerbating your pooch's condition since it won't be anywhere near the neck, unlike a collar that wraps around it.

Frontclip harnesses are a new form of harness for dogs that allow owners to attach the leash to their dogs' chest, preventing their dogs from pulling them along while out and about.

If a collar is okay for your Goldendoodle, you can choose from the common designs; namely, buckle/quick-connect, safety/breakaway, limited-slip/greyhound/martingale, and head halter.

Specifically designed for dogs with long fur, buckle/quick-connect collars can be flat or rolled. They typically attach via a buckle or plastic fastener. Apart from being a good first choice as your Goldendoodle's collar for training, a buckle/quick-connect collar makes a nice daily collar.

Designed to prevent choking, breakaway/safety collars feature a release that lets them spring open when pressure is applied to them. The safety release becomes inactive when a leash is attached to the collar.

Limited-slip/martingale/greyhound collars are named so because they are often used on greyhounds and other dog breeds that have heads and necks measuring the same diameter. They tighten a little when pressure is applied. They feature a mechanical stop that limits how much they tighten. This prevents choking and slipping.

Like a horse's halter, head halters wrap around the bridge of a dog's nose as well as the back of your dog's head. The leash attaches under the jaw. Such a design discourages the dog from pulling on the leash by enabling his or her owner to turn the head from side to side easily. Thus, head halters are commonly used by owners to train their dogs to behave while walking if a regular collar doesn't work.

Leashes are a way to keep pets under control. They are available in various materials, lengths, and widths. Lighter materials and smaller widths are commonly used on small dogs. Heavier materials and larger widths are commonly used on bigger dogs. Most leashes feature hardware that attaches to a collar or harness.

The two main types of leashes are standard and retractable. Standard leashes are typically made of leather, nylon or cotton, as well as measure 4-6 feet. These are recommended for both training and daily use since they are pretty straightforward.

Retractable leashes consist of a cord, a plastic case, and a handle. The cord automatically rolls up into the case by pushing the button. These are useful for training a dog to walk or exercise at a distance. Use one only after fully training your Goldendoodle since they can be unsafe if handled improperly.

Aside from serving as your Goldendoodle's very own spot to rest and hang out, a crate helps you house-train your pet as well as keeps them safe when he or she is unsupervised. You can choose between a wire or plastic crate. The former is sturdier and provides your Goldendoodle more ventilation. The latter is easier to clean and gives your pooch more privacy. If your dog is a heavy chewer, opt for a crate made of heavy-gauge wire. If you plan to take your pet on a lot of trips, also get a fabric crate with soft sides to make sure your dog stays comfortable in your car. If you got a puppy, make sure the crate will still fit him or her when he or she grows up. You can put in a divider to block off the rear until it reaches full size. Make sure your pet has enough space to lie down, turn around and get up without his or her head hitting the top. If you're unsure which equipment is right for him or her, consult a professional trainer, who can give you credible advice.

CHAPTER 10

Having Fun with Your Goldendoodle: How Can We Enjoy Time Together but Stay Safe?

Playing with your Goldendoodle isn't all, well, fun and games. Not only do you need to keep yourself and your new pet safe; you also need to be careful when around other people and pets. To help ensure both of you remain free from harm but still enjoy yourselves, this chapter teaches you what games are okay and not okay to play at home or indoors; how to go about playing with other people and pets outdoors; and what are the dos and don'ts for giving your pooch toys.

Having Fun at Home: What Games Are Okay and Not Okay?

Like most dog breeds, Goldendoodles also need regular playtime.

While it may sound strange, playing with your Goldendoodle, whether indoors or outdoors, is better for him or her if it isn't completely about having fun.

Dogs need exercise every day. They need to be walked several times each day no matter what the weather is like.

What do you do if you can't go out? Here are some indoor games that will give your Goldendoodle a physical and mental workout

- **Let your Goldendoodle run up and down the stairs.** This is an effective way to tire out your dog if you must stay inside. Indeed, having to go up and down several inclined steps is a more strenuous exercise than a usual walk or run. To turn this into a game, stand at the top of the stairs and throw one of your pooch's toys down at your pet. When they grab it, have them bring you the toy. Repeat until both of you are content.

- **Set up an obstacle course.** Gather the things you need, plot out where to put them around the house to make them look like an obstacle course, and lead your Goldendoodle through it. For example, you can make your dog jump through your old hula hoop and then crawl through some of your cushions that you've turned into a tunnel.

- **Play hide-and-seek using some dog treats.** Take a handful of your Goldendoodle's dog biscuits and hide them around the house for your furry friend to find. Tracking them down is a great way for your dog stay active and alert indoors.

- **Walk your Goldendoodle on your treadmill if you have one.** This lets your pet enjoy the health benefits of being walked even if you can't go outside.

The steps

- Switch on your treadmill and set it to its lowest speed but don't put your Goldendoodle on it yet. Let your dog get comfortable with the sight and sound of your treadmill when it's running first, so your pet doesn't get stressed out.

- Switch off your treadmill and then place your Goldendoodle on it. Give it a treat, so it stays.

- Once your Goldendoodle is relaxed, switch on your treadmill and set it to its lowest speed once more.

- Give your Goldendoodle more treats so it doesn't get off. If your pet makes it difficult, use his or her leash. But don't tie your dog to the treadmill to avoid any accidents. You can also stand in front of the treadmill and reward your dog with treats for walking and to it settle down and obey.

- Once your dog has adjusted, you can begin gradually increasing the speed to give your pooch a more challenging workout if you like.

Keep in mind that not all games are okay to play with your Goldendoodle inside. One of the riskiest is a tug-of-war. It can bring out the predator instinct in your Goldendoodle. This can be dangerous if he or she hasn't been house-trained yet or have behavioral issues.

That said, you won't have to stop yourself from playing tug-of-war forever if you want to. Just make sure you have established control over your Goldendoodle before doing so.

Also, remember to keep your Goldendoodle indoors and play with your dog for only appropriate lengths of time. Apart from socialization, dogs need limitations. Playing inside with your Goldendoodle too much could make your dog dislike playing outdoors and with other pets. This prevents your dog from meeting other people and pets as well as getting outdoor exercise, both of which your dog needs to stay healthy.

Having Fun Outdoors: How Do We Play Around Other People and Pets?

Playing with your Goldendoodle outdoors can be complicated. There are many factors you need to consider. You have to keep your pooch under control, know how to approach and play with other people and pets, and be able to keep a close eye on your pet when your dog is about or playing with the other dogs. Of course, you need to make sure you have fun. Here are tips to help you out.

- **If your Goldendoodle is a Mini/Toy/Teacup/Petite Goldendoodle, keep your dog away from or out of the play area for large dogs.** Not all places have separate play areas. If you take your Mini/Toy/Teacup/Petite Goldendoodle to such a place, know that your dog can be viewed as prey by the large dogs there. His or her squeaky barks and darting movements if it gets uncomfortable, nervous, afraid or agitated can trigger the natural prey drive in large dogs and lead to a disastrous confrontation.

- **Don't pick up your Mini/Toy/Teacup/Petite Goldendoodle either.** From a dog's point of view, something that goes up quickly is running away to the top of a tree. This triggers his or her instinct to chase. In other words, it triggers their doggie prey drive. All excited, he or she could jump onto you to get at your Goldendoodle. You could get knocked over, drop your pooch, lose them as she runs away from the worked-up dog, or get bitten.

- **Don't let your Goldendoodle bully the other dogs.** While it's adorable to see your furry friend bouncing all over another dog or the other dogs, be careful that this isn't actually your wonderful dog from being rude or obnoxious. Friendly gestures, like a play bow from a little distance away and a tag-and-run invitation, are okay. Incessantly nipping at another dog's ears and pouncing on the other dog to provoke play isn't especially appreciated if the other dog doesn't like it. If your pooch is getting too rough, call your dog over and tell him to stop. The dogs could end up fighting, or the other dog's owner could yell at you and your pooch otherwise.

- **Don't let the dogs 'work it out' among themselves.** While they are capable of this, if it's their first-time meeting and it's in a stimulating environment, like a park, where there are lots of other things that can excite them, their owners need to intervene so nothing bad happens. Say your Goldendoodle tries to mount another dog to show his or her dominance and you and the owner of the other dog ignore this as just your pet figuring out the hierarchy but the other dog doesn't like it. A fight is sure to break out between them, so separate them and take your dog to another area.

Giving Your Goldendoodle Toys: What Are the Dos and Don'ts?

Giving your Goldendoodle toys can make his or her playtime even more enjoyable. But if you unwittingly or mistakenly give your pet inappropriate toys, which might hurt your pet or it might get sick, or worse.

Here are things you need to keep in mind when choosing toys for your Goldendoodle to ensure you pick not only appropriates ones but the best ones for your pet to remain safe and sound while playing.

- **Make sure the toys are the right size for your Goldendoodle.** If he or she is a Mini/Toy/Teacup/Petite Goldendoodle, avoid buying toys that are too big. Your pet won't be able to carry these in its mouth, making it difficult for your pet to be playing with. If your dog is a large-breed Goldendoodle, or his or her parent is a large-breed Golden Retriever, toys that are too small can be choking hazards.

- **Avoid getting your Goldendoodle fetch toys that are too hard or too heavy.** An extremely hard fetch toy can break teeth when your pooch tries to catch it. If it's excessively heavy, it can hurt the head or neck.

- **Take extra care with tug toys.** There are tug toys that are long enough to wrap around your Goldendoodle's limbs and neck, so if you got your dog one, take it out only when you're there to take charge. Playing with it excessively or inappropriately can also exacerbate your Goldendoodle's neck or back or issues if he or she has such problems, so consult a veterinarian before getting one for your furry friend.

- **Avoid buying your Goldendoodle toys with string or other similar long, thin parts.** Your furry friend could eat or swallow these, causing gastrointestinal problems.

- **Avoid chew toys made of rawhide.** While such toys are traditionally made of this material, it tends to break apart over time especially if the dogs that play with them are strong chewers. If they are also quick eaters, the pieces of rawhide they ingest can become intestinal blockages. Rawhide itself can also get contaminated and cause an infection if consumed.

- **Consider stuffing-free toys.** These are safe compared to stuffed toys since virtually all dogs like to rip stuffing out of toys which can cause dogs gastrointestinal distress if ingested. It's okay to get your Goldendoodle stuffed toys as long as they don't get to the stuffing or ingest it. But this is easier said than done, so get your puppy stuffing-free toys instead.

- **Avoid battery-operated toys.** If your Goldendoodle tends to gnaw on toys and you got some battery-operated toys, your pet can puncture the batteries, unwittingly swallow the toxic substances inside and get sick, or worse. If your dog isn't this tough on his or her toys, you can get him or her battery-operated toys as long as you keep a close eye out while they play with those toys. But, like keeping your dog from ingesting the stuffing of stuffed toys, this is quite hard, so reconsider the purchase instead.

- **Make sure you get your Goldendoodle chew toys made of nontoxic materials.** Read the list of constituent parts carefully to ensure the rubber or plastic doesn't contain any harmful chemicals, such as phthalates, or BPA.

Conclusion

An amiable, affectionate, lively and fun-loving temperament. High intelligence which makes training it virtually no trouble at all. Adorableness mainly due to having a delightful, relatively hypoallergenic coat which can be fluffy or velvety and kinky, wavy, ragged or smooth.

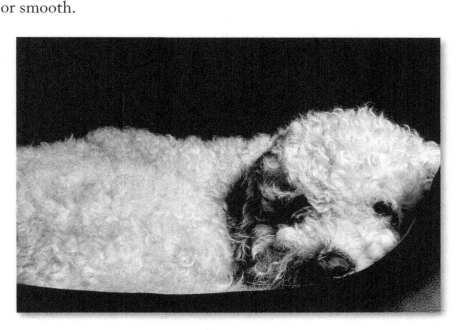

Amiable, affectionate, lively and fun-loving temperament,
training a Goldendoodle is no trouble.

These are but only some of the several things that make the Goldendoodle one of the currently most popular dog breeds. It's no surprise then that you've decided to have a Goldendoodle as your new beloved pet.

So, the process of making the Goldendoodle you have your heart set on part of your life turns out well, bear in mind the things you need to do to choose the right type of Goldendoodle for you. Take care of your fluffy friend as best you can, and properly train your dog.

It starts before you set out to find the perfect Goldendoodle for you. You need to prepare. This involves Goldendoodle-proofing your home, finding out what type of dog food is best for your soon-to-be pet, and getting the necessary gear to care for your pooch.

To make your pet feel even more welcome when he or she arrives, you also need to get your Goldendoodle a gift, or a few.

On the day of his or her arrival, remember the things you need to do to properly introduce your Goldendoodle to your family or other pet(s) as well as ensure your new pet settles in nicely in his or her new home as early as the first day.

If you got yourself a Goldendoodle puppy, keep in mind the several things you need to do to raise your dog properly, including crate and potty training. If you got a growing or adult Goldendoodle, make sure you do the things that let both of you adjust to each other along with your family or other pet(s) well.

You also need to make sure that you do all the important things to take care of your Goldendoodle the right away, including keeping your pet on a diet that's balanced. Ensuring your dog always eats healthy food, keeping your dog looking good by regularly grooming, keeping your furry friend fit through sufficient exercise, and doing preventive health maintenance to keep your dog from getting sick, are all top priorities.

Taking care of your Goldendoodle doesn't mean just tending to doggie needs. This also involves training of your dog. Make sure you go through the entire process. Teach your dog all of the easy, mid-level and hard tricks that all dogs need to learn to be good, reliable and even more adorable. To assure your training of your Goldendoodle turns out successfully, use the right training gear. Remember how to choose the best ones to ensure your precious pooch gets properly trained.

After taking care of the serious stuff, it could be tempting just to let your Goldendoodle play and have as much fun as your pet wants with hardly any supervision. It's better to keep everything under control whether you're having fun indoors, outdoors, or with other people or pet(s) to avoid having any accidents, so remember the things you need to do to stay safe and sound but still have fun.

By being a responsible pet owner, you and your Goldendoodle are sure to enjoy lots of fun years together.

Made in the USA
Monee, IL
18 August 2020